UNDERSTANDING STRESS

a Consumer Publication

edited by   Edith Rudinger

published by   Consumers' Association
publishers of **Which?**

Which? Books are commissioned and researched
by The Association for Consumer Research
and published by Consumers' Association,
2 Marylebone Road, London NW1 4DX and
Hodder and Stoughton, 47 Bedford Square,
London WC1B 3DF

© Consumers' Association Ltd April 1988

ISBN 0 85202 368 5
and   0 340 41622 X

Photoset by Paston Press, Loddon, Norfolk
Printed by Page Bros. (Norwich) Ltd.

UNDERSTANDING STRESS

a Consumer Publication

Consumers' Association
publishers of **Which?**
2 Marylebone Road
London NW1 4DX

CONTENTS

Foreword   7

Living with stress   9
some bodily reactions, physiological response, some physical symptoms: pain, palpitations and chest discomfort, fainting, choking, indigestion and nausea, diarrhoea, frequency of urination, tremor and twitching, tiredness, insomnia, breathlessness, overbreathing, better breathing, tension headaches and muscle aches, massage

Recognising the warning signs   32
change in eating pattern, increase in smoking, change in sleeping pattern, increased drinking and alcohol dependence

Life events   40
the stress chart

Illness and death   42
handicapping illness, facing death, bereavement and grief

Stress in marriage   47
choice of partner, sex, having children, quarrelling and conflict, seeking help, aggression in the family

Stress in childhood   57
birth of new baby, school, adolescence

Family stress   63

Stress in divorce   64
a kind of mourning, the children, loneliness

Growing older   73

The world around us   76
noise, driving and traffic, holidays and travel, crime, prison entence

Stress at work   86
factors intrinsic in the job, the organisation, women, employer/employee, workaholics, unemployment, retirement

Stress-related diseases 99
allergy, angina pectoris, asthma, cancer, diabetes, heart attack, hypertension, irritable bowel syndrome, migraine, peptic ulcer, premenstrual tension, rheumatoid arthritis, skin diseases, tinnitus

Anxiety and depression 116
abnormal anxiety states, phobias, abnormal depressive states, anti-depressant, tranquillisers, drug dependence, suicide

The general practitioner 129
the team, alternative and complementary therapies

Help from others 134
counselling, psychotherapy

Helping oneself 142
personality factors, ways of coping, religious activities

Learning to relax 155
progressive relaxation, meditation, autogenic training, hypnotherapy, biofeedback

Exercise and recreation 167
yoga, T'ai-chi, improving your health, hobbies, laughter and singing

Index 174

Useful organisations are listed throughout the book with the symbol Ø and can also be looked up in the Index. When writing to an organisation for information, please enclose a stamped self-addressed envelope.

FOREWORD

The aspect of stress which interests most people is the relation-ship to illness. Can stress cause illness? If so, which illnesses? As a corollary, can illness be treated by lessening or avoiding stress? If so, which illnesses?

However, before these questions can be answered, one must attempt to define the meaning of the term. It refers to pressures on a person that are seen in some way as excessive, perhaps intolerable. It also refers to the psychological and physical changes in response to those pressures. Con-sequently, the term stress has become imprecise in scientific terms although most lay people seem to be familiar with the concepts involved.

In this book, stress is described and related to various periods and events in a person's life. The stresses during adolescence are obviously different from those during adult-hood which in turn differ from the problems encountered by the elderly. The responses of the individual are detailed, both with respect to psychological effects such as anxiety and depression and bodily effects such as the release of excess adrenaline into the bloodstream.

An important section deals with the disorders believed to be particularly bound up with stress responses such as asthma, high blood pressure and peptic ulcer. Other conditions in which the relationship is less clear are outlined.

Stress is not always apparent: sometimes the pressures in one's life can be quite subtle but still considerable. In these instances the individual may find changes in his behaviour which puzzle him. A section of the book covers ways of realising where stress is impinging increasingly on one's life. Considerable space is devoted to ways of combating stress by self-help, learning to cope and by seeking help from medical and other agencies. Advice is given about smoking, drinking and drugs and how to avoid excessive reliance on them. Methods of relaxation are described together with ways of taking stress out of everyday activities.

This book is an excellent introduction to this wide topic and also provides useful, practical and sensible advice. Everyone who feels stressed or suspects a friend or relative to be stressed can benefit from reading it and will find it easier to help themselves and others.

Professor Malcolm Lader

Institute of Psychiatry
University of London

LIVING WITH STRESS

A bit of stress is part of normal life, and is not necessarily always bad. Even joyful events, such as marriage, a birth, a new job, can be stressful because of the changes they entail in the person's life.

With no stress, no pressure or demands on us, it would be hard to get going at all, and many people would lack motivation. Too much stress is bad, but so is too little.

Stress is inherent in the human condition and our century has intensified many stresses and added new ones, many of them psychological or social in nature. Since stress cannot be avoided, it has to be managed and coped with.

One man's mild stimulation from life is another man's intolerable burden. What is severe stress to me, may be no more than a tiresome or niggling incident to you. The degree of stress is determined not only by external events but also by how a person perceives the events and responds to them. There are few absolute sources of stress: the interaction between a potential source of stress and the person's own attitudes and vulnerabilities determines whether a situation is experienced as stressful.

In general, stress refers to pressures on an individual that are in some way perceived as excessive, or intolerable, and also to the psychological and physical changes in response to those pressures.

Some stresses are related to, or follow on, a specific identifiable event in the person's life. Attempts have been made to list life events in order of severity of their stressful impact. Death of one's spouse is usually ranked first, followed by divorce and marital separation, imprisonment, death of a close relative (especially a parent or child). Personal injury and illness, loss of employment or retirement, acute sex difficulties, and change in health of a family member come next. Even planned or eagerly awaited events such as going on holiday, a wanted pregnancy, retirement, are regarded as having a stressful impact.

Life events which are less important in terms of stress include change in financial state, death of a close friend, taking out a mortgage, change of job or of responsibilities, and in-law troubles. Other life events related to stress are one's spouse stopping or starting work and minor offences such as traffic violations.

Some life events are unpredictable and the person has no control at all, such as death of a spouse or personal injury; some stresses are brought on by the individual himself, such as taking out a loan to buy a new car.

range of problems

The trouble starts when several life events hit you all at once. People are more vulnerable to stress during periods of major change. There is a finite number of changes that any individual can handle at any one time, and usually the straw which breaks the camel's back is unpredictable. Therefore, where there is a predictable life event looming, you should try not to make things worse by introducing other changes in your life – such as changing jobs and getting married at the same time.

It is not easy to lessen stress when a person faces a whole range of problems rather than one identifiable difficulty. Moreover, people under a lot of stress are less able to cope. This in turn leads to more stress and less ability to cope – and a vicious circle sets in.

Stress responses involve many bodily symptoms, emotional reactions and behavioural changes and yet many people drift into situations in which the level of stress rises insidiously, and do not seem to realise what is happening.

Most of us come across stresses every day but only rarely do we get stress symptoms or stress related illnesses. What seems to be important is not just the number or seriousness of stressors but also under what context they occur, our attitudes, beliefs, expectations, the physical, psychological, social climate in which we live and our own susceptibility. Problems at home are not left behind when people go to work. They play on the mind and create a complex interaction. Even the political situation can have health implications: worries about standards of schools for our children, welfare benefit, chances of employment, or a boring job, or unemployment, the amount of taxes we have to pay. Poor housing conditions, a poor nutritional state, limited resources, make people specially vulnerable.

recognising stress

The key issue is not how stress can be avoided, but how it can be coped with to advantage. Stress is often thought of as only bad; people fail to see that it can be a positive force in their lives.

The secret is to find one's optimum level of stress. This varies from person to person and also varies in ourselves from one day to the next. Each of the different areas of satisfaction in life – work, study, family, marriage, relationships, social activities, leisure, sport – carries its own stresses. Such stresses can sometimes even help to develop latent resources. You may find that you can tolerate higher levels of stress in some areas than in others, and may even actively seek them.

Not only does reducing stress to tolerable levels lead to a more consistent or greater sense of well-being, it also reduces the likelihood of some physical illnesses. There is a close link between processes in the body and processes in the mind. Stress influences both of them, and some illnesses are regarded by some doctors as specifically stress-related. Stress can be the cause of some illness, it can make others worse, and is involved in the mechanism of yet many others.

some bodily reactions to stress

In the animal world, the response to acute stress or alarm (such as is produced by the appearance of a predator or other threat) is to fight or flee, or – more rarely – to sit paralysed by fear.

The body responds to emotional stress as if it were physical stress, by preparing itself for fight or flight. Human reactions are not very different and involve very rapid, almost instant changes in the muscles and organs of the body.

The sense organs of sight or hearing receive the signal of alarm and pass it on to the brain from which messages are sent along the nerves to the muscles and to other organs. The muscles contract, often very abruptly; if the state of alertness or arousal continues, muscle activity and tension remain high to render the person more capable of reacting quickly to any further stimuli.

Heart rate tends to change: most people have felt their heart beating faster after a shock. Blood pressure sometimes rises to quite high levels and may remain high for some time. Under certain circumstances, such as anticipation of something unpleasant, the heart may slow down and beat very forcibly.

Blood vessels throughout the body are affected; those in the muscles open up, so that more blood can course through them; those in the abdomen and in the skin contract, so that less blood goes through them. Thus the output of the heart is diverted from skin and gut to the muscle of the trunk and limbs, in preparation for greater muscular effort.

Sweating increases in fairly specific areas such as the skin around the mouth and nose, the temples, the armpits, between the legs and, especially, the palms of the hands and the soles of the feet.

The saliva dries up. Secretion of gastric acid increases, the gastro-intestinal tract is markedly affected although movement of the stomach may diminish. Sometimes the stomach becomes flabby – literally, a 'sinking stomach'. The intestines are more active and may churn and gurgle. There may be an urge to open one's bowels and, in a severe fright, loss of control may occur. The bladder is affected similarly: there is an urge to pass water as the bladder muscle increases its activity.

The sensory organs alter. For example, the pupil of the eye dilates, so letting in more light and functioning in a more sensitive manner.

hormones

Hormonal changes are less immediate because their speed is determined by the rate of the blood's circulation round the body. Hormones are chemical substances which are secreted into the blood stream by glands in various places throughout the body and travel in the blood stream to their particular sites of action.

Of the many hormones implicated in stress responses, the most important ones are adrenaline and noradrenaline (known collectively as the adrenomedullary hormones) and cortisol or hydrocortisone (an adrenocortical hormone). Different species of animals secrete adrenaline and noradrenaline in different proportions; in man, it is mainly adrenaline.

Adrenaline and noradrenaline which are secreted into the bloodstream act on many organs, in general reinforcing the effects. It is through them that heart rate increases, blood pressure rises, the pupils dilate, blood flow in the muscle increases, blood flow to skin and gut diminishes and the breathing tubes (bronchi) expand, allowing more air to be drawn into the lungs. In addition, adrenaline affects the metabolic balance of the body. It mobilises energy reserves in the liver and in the muscles themselves, making glucose available for immediate energy demands.

physiological response

These changes are accompanied by changes in posture which indicate increased alertness. The person's body is in a state of readiness to respond to any further stimuli.

The likely sequence of events might have been: primitive man sees lion → increased stimulation by the sympathetic nervous system and increased adrenaline and noradrenaline release → increased heart rate → increased blood flow to vital organs and muscles → man equipped to grapple with lion or, if more sensible, to make a hasty retreat. In civilised man, neither action is very likely, so that the response, in terms of increase in heart rate, muscle tensing and other physiological changes is, in fact, inappropriate. The sequence of events in this day and age is more likely that man hears telephone rining in office → intense business argument → increased adrenaline and noradrenaline release → increased heart rate → increased blood flow to muscles → man equipped to grapple physically with business opponent but does not do so, or at least not usually. And so an apparently wasted series of physiological events has occurred. The latent urge for some physical outlet may be externalised by fierce beating of the first on the desk.

Each person has individual patterns of physiological and psychological response to stimuli and the pattern of responses will tend to be similar whenever a stimulus recurs. Thus, in one person the pulse rate may markedly increase each time, but there is little sweating; another person may show the reverse pattern with marked sweat-gland responses. One person's response is raised blood pressure, another's is increased secretion of gastric acid, a third shows much muscle tension, and so on.

adapting

If the same stimuli are repeated, the responses fall off to some extent because there is adaptation or habituation. This is a very basic form of learning – learning not to respond to stimuli which after some repetition are consciously or unconsciously perceived as irrelevant. The fall-off in response tends to be rapid at first, then tails off. Adaptation is a complex matter and its mechanism in warding off the effects of stress is not fully known.

People vary greatly in the rate at which they adapt to repeated stimuli. Some do so rapidly, ceasing to respond after a short time; others very slowly or not at all. Some unfortunates actually become increasingly susceptible: each exposure to the stimulus increases their response. Through failure to adapt, readiness and arousal are kept at a quite unnecessarily high level. It has been suggested that a failure to adapt can turn into stresses many stimuli which are in themselves fairly innocuous.

When a stimulus becomes invested with a special significance, this can reverse the process of adaptation. For example, someone living near an airport may have learned not to be troubled by the noise of aircraft flying overhead. Then he reads of a near-collision in the air, becomes sensitised to aircraft noise and, thereafter, aircraft noise constitutes a stress for him.

When a repeated stress no longer induces a bodily response, nor produces an emotional reaction, by definition, it is no longer a stress. Nevertheless, it is possible that the stressful circumstances are still registered by the person, even if not responded to, and this may eventually produce changes in the body, for instance changes in sensitivity of hormonal control mechanisms.

some physical symptoms

Sometimes stressful circumstances can give rise to symptoms of physical distress, pain or malfunctioning. If the stress response is not recognised for what it is and is regarded as a possible sign of physical illness, this can cause a great deal of needless worry.

Stress can produce a tremendous varieity of physical symptoms and any part of the body can be upset. Chest discomfort or pain, diarrhoea, palpitations, headaches, muscle twitches may all be signs of an increase in stress. Chronic pains become worse and more unbearable. The stressed person complains more of his symptoms and may become querulous or importune his doctor for reassurance and remedies. Multiple complaints in a hitherto stoic person may be the first sign of increasing stress.

pain

Pain is a subjective sensation and can be affected by previous experience of pain. Some people can tolerate a lot of pain and others only a little. Under stress, some of us may become anxious, hypochondriacal or depressed. Minor physical complaints may be magnified in the person's mind, consciously or unconsciously, until they produce a quite disproportionate disability.

Pain can become genuinely worse when a person has causes for anxiety, such as worry about illness or physical disorder. An upset in personal relationships, job worries, a bereavement, or being under financial pressure can affect the symptoms. For instance, backache can become worse as a result of psychological stress, anxiety, and other social and emotional pressures.

Prolonged persistent pain can itself be a profoundly disturbing experience and very stressful. If it goes on long enough, it may disturb the normal pattern of behaviour.

palpitations and chest discomfort

The 'resting' heart rate averages between 60 and 80 beats per minute, but the rate can rise to as high as 200 beats per minute during extreme exercise or under stress. The word palpitations means no more than that one is aware of the beating (normal or abnormal) of one's heart. This is quite usual, for instance, during and immediately after exercise.

Palpitations can be caused by additional contractions of the heart (which make the individual feel as if his heart has 'turned over') called ectopic beats. This is quite a common condition and the majority of people who experience it have a healthy heart; in some people, it is set off by anxiety or stress – but excessive coffee or tea drinking or alcohol and other causes may do so more often.

Chest discomfort and pain are common complaints in stressful situations and anxious people. The pain is an ache (rather than the constricting sensation of angina or a heart attack) or it may be a stabbing pain felt over the heart. Although these pains may be provoked by exertion, they tend to last longer than angina pains which disappear after exertion has ceased. However, a doctor's expertise may be needed to make the distinction between these harmless symptoms of stress and those of true coronary heart disease.

Living in doubt can cause further anxiety which can be very exhausting and can, in turn, produce further symptoms. So, if you have any chest pains, go and see your doctor.

The combination of these stress pains and such stress symptoms as tiredness, weakness, sweating, trembling and breathlessness (especially breathlessness at rest) has been given various names such as effort syndrome, disordered action of the heart, cardiac neurosis. It responds to the relief of the pain, reassurance from a qualified person that there is no heart disease, and treatment directed to the source of the stress.

fainting

Under acute emotional stress, some people faint or fear they are going to faint: they feel light-headed and may experience palpitations and sweaty palms and may then pass out – that is, become unconscious. This is due to a change in the nervous control of the blood vessels, some of which widen, and of the heart rate so that it beats less frequently and less vigorously. As a result, the blood pressure falls and the circulation through the brain becomes insufficient. If the sufferer is laid horizontal or, while still conscious, puts his head down between his knees, he will recover within a few minutes. He should not be put into an upright sitting or standing position.

choking

Under stress, or great excitement, some people suffer from a sensation of choking. Because the mouth is dry from lack of saliva and the muscles of the throat are taut, they feel that the tongue is blocking the air passage. Actually it never does, although speech may be thick and difficult. The symptom usually subsides quickly when the acute stress is relieved.

indigestion and nausea

Some people suffer vague abdominal pains under stress. These pains are fairly diffuse, unlike an ulcer pain, and are generally not relieved by indigestion remedies. Make a note of when the pain comes on – it may reveal a pattern that will help to identify the source of the stress.

In many people, the gut does not respond with a specific symptom immediately after a stress, but the background of stress may lead to gastro-intestinal symptoms.

Nausea is a common symptom in relation to stress (particularly in an anxious person). The person may not be able to face anything to eat or drink in the morning, for the first couple of hours after getting up. As the day wears on, the appetite improves and the feeling of nausea disappears. Nausea with pain may be due to a disease, such as peptic ulcer, but painless nausea may simply be due to being under stress.

diarrhoea and frequency of urination

Under acute stress, such as is experienced by soldiers going into battle, overactivity of the gut can result in diarrhoea. Responding to stress with diarrhoea may happen in isolation or it may alternate with constipation. Such physiological symptoms, however, should not necessarily be attributed only to stress. They may be signs of some serious condition and, if they persist, the doctor should be consulted.

The bladder is another organ which reacts to stress, the person having to pass urine more frequently than usual. The urge to pass urine may be very sudden and sometimes minor incontinence may occur. But incontinence may also be caused by a serious underlying illness, so if it persists you should consult your doctor.

tremor and twitching

The muscular system of the body is under very finely tuned controls. Under stress, the control mechanisms can become inefficient because of interference by impulses coming from the complex centres of the brain which govern the emotions. In addition, adrenaline which is released into the bloodstream can induce such changes. The result is trembling – mainly of the hands, but it can affect any part of the body. Some people who normally suffer from tremor are made worse by stress and anxiety. The trembling can be marked and disabling.

Tremor of the voice muscles is shown as shakiness of the voice, or whispering. Stammering, which is a complex malfunctioning of the control and the monitoring of speech production, is made worse by stress.

Twitching, another muscular stress response, may affect a tiny muscle such as one at the corner of the mouth or eye. This twitch may be so highly related to stress or anger as to be an external indicator of the sufferer's state of mind (or body).

tiredness

Prolonged stress and prolonged emotion, even when enjoyable, usually lead to a feeling of tiredness, which people may describe as feeling drained. People differ considerably in the speed with which this happens. Although the sufferer often feels worn out physically as well as mentally, this tiredness has probably more to do with mental tension than with fatigue of the muscles or other parts of the body. A good long night's sleep or two may be all that is needed. If the tiredness continues, you should consider discussing the matter with your doctor to make sure that there is no medical reason for it. A longer period of mental rest, relaxation and diversion into other interests may be all that is required.

In the magazine *Self-Health* for March 1987 a 'tiredness' chart is accompanied by the warning that "Lethargy is a common symptom of many disorders, some trivial and some that require medical treatment. Sudden severe drowsiness is a serious symptom and requires prompt medical attention."

insomnia

Many middle-aged and older people, particularly those of anxious temperament who carry a sense of responsibility, will have to accept that for years they will fell their sleep to be less good than they would like.

Sleep problems at any age can take various forms: difficulty in getting to sleep, waking in the night, waking early, unsatisfactory sleep.

Difficulty in getting to sleep is characteristically related to anxiety, not being able to switch off problems when going to bed; the person tosses and turns and finds it increasingly difficult to fall asleep. When sleep does come, it is unsatisfying in nature often with anxiety-provoking dreams, or even nightmares, of frightening situations, running away and trying to escape, and the dreamer wakes bathed in sweat.

Fitful and disturbed sleep, waking frequently in the night, is typically related to depression, so is waking early to gloomy thoughts.

Insomnia due to anxiety or depression, or to stress, is unlikely to be relieved until these states of mind have been dealt with. Moreover, inadequate sleep can be a contributing factor in stress, so it would be wise to try and tackle the insomnia directly.

Try to discover whether your sleeping problem really is a problem at all. People who believe they have chronic insomnia may be getting only about forty minutes less sleep than 'normal' people. Or you could explore your sleep problem with a relative or friend, or with your GP. The change in your sleeping habits might even have been brought about by drugs prescribed for some illness.

In some cases, sleeping pills could be useful in seeing someone through a bad period of stress on a short-term basis. But sleeping pills do not do anything to deal with the cause of insomnia, particularly if this is, for example, pain or some physical illness. Treatment for relief of the pain should also improve your sleep.

how to sleep better

If it is the environment – noise, someone else in the room, light, heat or cold – which makes sleep more difficult, some simple measures are worth trying. You may not be able to get the noise stopped, so try earplugs for a short time or, to lessen traffic noise, consider installing double glazing; if light comes from the street, use thick lined curtains or blinds; get the temperature right by opening windows or switching on a heater.

The body clock works to a 24-hour cycle, so it is wise to go to bed at about the same time every night and to avoid constantly changing sleep times (it may mean having to give up shift-work, or frequent travel).

It is also wise always to get up at the same time each morning. Generally, if people get up regularly at the same hour, the hour when they get sleepy at night tends to look after itself. Some people who feel they cannot get to sleep at night try to make up for it by lying around longer in bed in the morning – and then have difficulty in falling asleep at night: a vicious circle.

It can be helpful to follow a night-time routine – such as taking the dog, or yourself, for a walk (particularly if you have been sitting most of the day); listening to the radio or reading (but avoid highly emotional topics, or carrying out over-stimulating intellectual tasks right up to bed-time); making a warm drink (not a stimulant such as coffee or tea and do not have a heavy meal late at night); having a bath, making sure you go to bed with an empty bladder.

There are some relaxation techniques which work by distracting you from whatever may be worrying you so that, once you are in bed, your body can relax and your mind drift off. Some methods occupy the mind – for example, making up stories, word games or simple adding or multiplication games, reciting poetry. Others involve clogging the brain with boring repetition such as counting sheep. Physical relaxation exercises, such as tensing and then relaxing different groups of muscles around the body and deep breathing can help towards better sleep. Sex, too, can help sleep.

breathlessness

To feel breathless following exercise is normal, but anxiety and stress can also produce a kind of breathlessness. This breathlessness is a feeling of suffocation, as though not being able to get a deep enough breath into the lungs. It is often accompanied by a habit of sighing. The sufferer has usually taken in a deep breath, is afraid to let it out, and breathes shallowly and rather rapidly. He should be reassured that he will not choke and should let his breath right out and then breathe in and out more deeply, but not fast. He can then also train himself not to indulge in tragic-sounding sighs.

overbreathing (hyperventilation)

There are two levels of breathing: chest breathing (thoracic) and diaphragmatic – the diaphragm is a muscular partition separating the thorax from the abdomen. Chest breathing occurs in arousal; relaxed breathing is slower and involves the diaphragm.

In conditions of stress, breathing may become quicker and shallower. In someone who tends towards overbreathing anyway, this response can become exaggerated at times of stress. He may feel that he cannot draw sufficient air into his lungs, and feel stifled. Some people may even trigger off panic attacks as they overbreathe.

The overbreathing, in blowing off carbon dioxide from the lungs, alters the metabolic balance of the body; the nerves become over-excitable, giving rise to symptoms such as pins and needles and tingling of the hands and feet. The person becomes more anxious, overbreathes more and a vicious circle is set up. The usual emergency treatment is for the sufferer to breathe into a paper bag so that he will re-inhale the carbon dioxide that he has just breathed out: the metabolic imbalance is thus corrected. After that, what has caused the stress response should be sought and dealt with, even though it may be trivial. This re-inhalation treatment is usually undertaken by doctors in hospitals, but a patient's relatives can be instructed to help.

In addition to (or, better, instead of) the paper bag routine, a person who overbreathes should be taught relaxed breathing by a chest physician or physiotherapist. Breathing patterns are not easily changed, but people can learn a better habit.

In some localities, classes on breathing and stress reduction are available at adult education institutes. The British Holistic Medical Association (179 Gloucester Place, London NW1 6DX, telephone 01-262 5299) sells a cassette on breathing and relaxation (£5 plus £1 postage).

better breathing
Most systems of relaxation include controlled breathing, generally deep breathing. Overbreathing under conditions of stress usually consists of breathing fast, or in pants and gasps; controlled deep breathing should be slow and steady. Slower, deeper breathing is a good and immediate way of altering mood, so as to feel calm rather than tense.

BREATHING EXERCISES

To practise better breathing, you should aim to fill the lower half of the lungs first, using the muscles of the rib cage and the diaphragm. Start by resting your hands against the bottom of the rib cage with the fingers lightly touching: if you breathe in correctly, you will find that your fingers will draw apart. Hold the breath for a short while, then let the muscles relax as you breathe out. Breathing should be rhythmical and there should be a constant ratio between the time spent breathing in and the time spent breathing out.

A good position for deep breathing is to lie on one's back, with the knees half bent and the hands over the lower chest with the fingers lightly meeting. As you breathe in, check that you are opening up and filling the lower part of the lungs (by observing how your fingers are drawn apart). As you breathe out, the fingers come together again.

Another way of checking that you are breathing correctly is to put one hand on the upper part of your chest and the other on your abdomen. You can do this sitting on a chair. When you breathe in, your abdomen should expand at the start of the breath and your upper chest should not move much. Repeat this exercise several times, aiming to get your abdomen moving (as evidenced by your lower hand).

What you should concentrate on is breathing out, fully and correctly (that is, slowly and evenly); then breathe in by simply allowing the air to come in naturally, with no exaggeration or conscious effort. It is the breathing out that is associated with relaxation of muscles and which can be used to assist general relaxation.

Calm controlled breathing can be used to counteract some of the stress in difficult situations, such as before an interview, an exam or a performance – or after a stressful row or a shock.

tension headaches and muscle aches

Muscles can go into sustained contraction during stress; the muscles of the scalp, neck and face are amongst the most vulnerable.

The basis of tension headache is sustained contraction of the muscles of the forehead and neck. The headache is generally insidious in onset, and gets worse during the day and may even become worse after the source of stress has lessened or been dealt with. It may be throbbing in character or, more likely, feel like a tight band round the head, all day long and every day. Or it may feel like a skull cap pulled down hard over the temples from the moment of waking until going to sleep. This may be not so much a pain but an awareness of discomfort. Stress or fatigue can accentuate the symptom. Taking analgesics (painkillers) usually helps, as does relaxation or massage.

Tooth clenching and grinding are stress-related habits; prolonged contraction of the muscles involved can cause headache and facial pain that seems like toothache. To help to counteract the tension of various facial muscles, try opening your mouth by about half an inch and pressing down the jaw against the pressure of a hand held under the chin, and then letting it drop normally. Do this for a few minutes each day, preferably in the evening before going to bed. But if the pain persists, go and see your dentist. Persistent tooth grinders may be able to obtain via the dentist a thin moulded plastic protector to fit over the teeth at night.

Muscle tension in other parts of the body can produce a variety of aches and pains, sometimes labelled 'fibrositis' which is a vague, convenient term for ill-defined pain in and around muscles. So-called 'lumbago' (low back pain), in particular, often becomes insistent and unbearable when the person becomes stressed.

Muscle tension can usually be clearly related to stressful circumstances, and can leave the person feeling physically exhausted at the end of the day.

Alexander technique

The Alexander technique is a method of relearning how to use muscles, to avoid tension by improving the awareness and use of the neuro-muscular mechanism which controls balance, movement and posture. Teachers of this method start by noting and correcting a pupil's characteristics patterns of body misuse and his faulty posture habits, which are creating physical and mental tension. The pupil is taught to recognise and apply the best pattern of movement and posture for him, and is then able to practise the method as a self-help technique. Students of the method find themselves gradually adopting better physical postures and also unwinding mentally.

Good posture helps good breathing and involves relaxing each part of the body.

Ø **The Society of Teachers of the Alexander Technique**, 10 London House, 266 Fulham Road, London SW10 9EL (telephone 01-351 0828) will, on request, send a list of teachers of the technique.

massage

Massage is useful in helping muscles to relax. It stimulates the flow of blood, assists in clearing away waste products from muscle cells and reduces muscular tension and associated pain.

Massage can also be valuable on an emotional plane. It is a form of physical contact between two people that can be very comforting; it reduces emotional tension and anxiety, and replaces them with a feeling of calm and trust. It can symbolise being cared for, friendship, affection and even tenderness. The person giving the massage also benefits, from the sense of touch and the satisfaction of helping someone in a direct personal way. Both parties should end up feeling relaxed and at peace.

Muscles cannot relax when cold, so it is better if the person who is being massaged is warm (and the room, too). The person who is giving the massage should not have cold hands. Rub your hands together to warm them before starting.

massaging

Before beginning the massage, place the hands on the partner and hold them still for a few seconds, so as to transmit a feeling of calm and to give you time to take some deep breaths to relax yourself. When the massage begins, it should not be tentative, but firm and deliberate. Do not remove both hands from the body at the same time, so as not to lose continuity. As you near the end of the massage, indicate this by a slight change of tempo and pressure. Leave your hands lying still on your partner for a little while, so that he can come to, gradually, in his own time. Right at the end, do some light strokes, imagining that you are 'dusting off' tension. Draw these strokes beyond the person's body.

You can, of course, massage any part of the body, but for stress the most effective parts are neck, shoulders and forehead. You should stand behind the person and lean forward a little, while he sits on a chair with his back to you and the head supported by resting against you. Shoulder massage can be done very effectively if the recipient is lying face down.

Because massage is such a useful and simple way of helping to deal with stress and tension, some physiotherapists or occupational therapists attached to GP clinics will instruct patients on how to do it, for example:

MASSAGE FOR SHOULDERS

Massage can be done sitting or lying. This sequence is for sitting.

Sit the person to be massaged, the receiver (R), on a dining-room type chair – sideways, if the chair has a high back where the shoulders would not be above the back of the chair if sitting conventionally.

1. Start by standing behind the receiver (R) and placing both hands, palms down on the shoulders. Your touch should be reassuring, firm, but not forced. Check that you and R are comfortable. Relax your breathing and wait until you have a sense that R is receptive to your touch.

2. Leave one hand resting on one shoulder, while you concentrate on working on the other side at the point where the neck and shoulders meet. Begin gently. Use your thumbs and fingers to make gentle circular movements to move the tissue. Gently knead and squeeze. Gradually work along the top of the shoulder towards the shoulder joint. Do gentle movements around the shoulder joint. Gradually loosen the tissue, not forcing, but gradually encouraging places of hardness and stuckness to loosen and relax. Ask for feedback. Too hard? Too soft? More? Less? etc. Pay special attention to the neck 'edge' and shoulder joint.

3. Now move to the part between the shoulder blade and spine. Continue using small circular movements to loosen the structures here. Feel for the little nooks and crannies. Work gently at first, and as R relaxes work more firmly and deeply.

4. Now continue with this circular stroke all over the shoulder blade, again loosening as before. Check that you yourself are relaxed; breathe.

5. Now repeat 2–4 on the other side of the back.

6. With both hands, gently 'brush off' the back. Imagine you are dusting off the surface of the back, sweeping dust particles as far away from R, into the air, as can be reached.

Do not work over the spine.

   Check frequently with R: massage should *not* be painful.

MASSAGE FOR NECK

1. There are three major bands of muscle on each side of the spine. Mentally divide the neck into three parts on the lefthand side of the spine and going round to the front of the neck, and similarly three parts on the righthand side.

2. Place both hands on R's shoulders. Wait, breathe and relax. Then leave one hand as support on the shoulder, and work on the opposite side.

3. Begin with the band of muscle of the neck nearest to the spine. Use fingers to do small, gentle, circular movements up the neck. Pay particular attention to the point where the neck meets the shoulders and where the neck meets the skull. Work gradually, gently to soften the structures in the neck.

4. Continue by doing these strokes up the middle band of that side of the neck.

5. Do the band of the neck round at the front.

6. Repeat 3–5 on the other side of the spine.

Do not massage over the spine, or over the wind-pipe at the front of the neck. Massage should not be painful; ask for feedback: is your partner comfortable? You may need to support your partner's forehead with one hand (not covering the eyes), or support at the opposite temple, instead of resting your other hand on the shoulder.

BACK OF THE HEAD MASSAGE
1. Ask your partner, the receiver (R) to let the head be relaxed. Support the forehead with one hand (not covering the eyes). Allow the head to tilt forward.

2. Begin on one side of the head. Feel the bony ridge where the skull meets the neck. Start from behind the ear, making small circular movements along, above and below the bony ridge. Gradually loosen the structures, not forcing; ask for feedback: too hard? Too soft? Too slow? Too fast?

3. When you get to the centre back of the head, pay special attention to the bony lump and hollow there. Continue doing small circular movements. Use fingers and thumb.

4. Change hands and support, and now work on the other side of the head.

5. To finish, using both hands and starting from the neck, brush upward along the neck and out of the head, imagining that you are brushing away lightly any loosened tension.

FRONT OF THE HEAD MASSAGE
1. Let your partner's head rest lightly backwards onto your chest. This enables you to use both hands sometimes. Check for comfort.

2. Start with the forehead. Mentally divide the forehead into three horizontal bands (lower, middle, upper). Use fingers/thumbs of both hands, starting just above the nose and between the eyes to smooth upwards across the skin. Take your

thumbs up and then out towards the temples, and then beyond the head. Imagine that you are pulling tension out and leaving it in the atmosphere. Repeat this several times. Then move on to the middle band of the forehead. Start again between the eyes, draw your fingers/thumbs up to the middle band, then towards the temples and out beyond the head. Repeat the process for the upper band. Then use your whole hand to cover the brow, and smooth across it several times, making sweeping movements with your hands, taking the movement beyond the head.

3. Use both hands, one on either side, to make circular movements with fingers or thumbs around the temples. Move the skin against the bone there. Be gentle. Then pull the tension out with your fingers in a movement going beyond the head.

4. On yourself, feel around the eye-socket. Locate the bony edges of the socket. Then on your partner, who should have the eyes closed, use a finger to press gently and then do a circular stroke along this edge. Be very gentle – the skin around the eyes is delicate. Repeat two or three times, then do the other eye socket. Finish by using the fingers to make feather-like strokes across both eyes and beyond the head.

5. Make small circular movements with fingers and thumbs from the corner of the eye down the side of the nose and down the laughter lines at the side of the mouth. Repeat several times. Do the other side. Then smooth the skin with both hands.

6. Either one side at a time or both together, work along the jaw from just below the ear round to the chin. Make small loosening circular movements. Pull tension out from the head.

7. Starting from the forehead or the chin, lightly stroke the whole face with both hands. Dust away loosened tension. Draw it away from the head.

8. Use both hands to make small circular movements all over the scalp – as in hairwashing.

9. Gently pull the hair. Draw tension away from the head.

10. Let your partner sit quietly for a while.

Now wash your hands.

The massage techniques can be done to oneself, basically anywhere one can reach such as shoulder, neck, face most other parts. (The back would be difficult.)

some hints on massage
○ Massage should never be painful.
○ Do not massage over infected sites, varicose veins, open wounds, swollen joints. If in doubt, don't.
○ Try to keep the rhythm of strokes smooth.
○ Always repeat strokes on both sides of the body.
○ Ask for feedback.
○ Make sure you and your partner are comfortable.
○ Try to concentrate on what you are doing. Do not let your attention wander.

recognising the warning signs

1 A person may recognise some of the signs of being under stress without being aware of the other ways in which stress is affecting him. He may find that he is sleeping poorly, but overlook the fact that he is smoking or drinking more; he may not appreciate that some other symptoms are also part of his stress response.

2 Each person tends to have his own pattern of stress response, so that warning signs of stress vary from person to person. There are many signs that a person is under stress.

3 One of the most obvious and early signs of stress to look out for in another person is an intensification of personality traits. The suspicious person becomes defensive. The careful becomes over-meticulous, the pessimistic lugubrious, the anxious panic-stricken, the inadequate falls to pieces altogether. The irritable becomes explosive, the extrovert becomes slapdash and the introspective loses contact with everyday reality.

Some people know their own pattern of stress response, and can gauge the depth of problems by the nature and severity of their own symptoms or changes in behaviour.

change in eating pattern

Some people lose their appetite when they become stressed, anxious and depressed; others eat more or even overeat when stressed, perhaps to comfort themselves. For some people, losing or putting on weight can be a barometer of their level of long-term stress. Loss and gain of weight may, however, be caused by something other, and perhaps more serious, than the decrease or increase of appetite, and should not be ignored.

Anorexia nervosa, a compulsive fasting which leads to physical illness, used to be almost entirely associated with teenage girls who saw themselves as too fat (when in fact they were not). More people, including men and older women are now seeking medical help for eating disorders. The causes are not clearcut but are often linked with stressful family relationships.

increase in smoking

Under stress, many smokers find the number of cigarettes they buy going up rapidly. The smoker takes great care to make sure that his supply of cigarettes does not run out. The need for a cigarette is never far from his mind, but often cigarettes are lit and smoked avidly for a few puffs and then stubbed out in an impatient, abrupt way.

Some smokers find their habit so sensitive to stress that they can gauge the stressfulness of a situation by their cigarette consumption.

Nicotine produces a complex series of changes in the body, including the release of adrenaline and noradrenaline, as in stress. So, smoking compounds the bodily effects of stress. Nicotine works fast – it takes only about 75 seconds between inhaling and the drug reaching the brain.

Cigarettes may help to lessen the emotional impact of stress, but at a high toll in medical consequences. The role of cigarette smoking in producing heart disease and lung cancer is well-known, but widely ignored by smokers.

People continue to smoke for any one of a number of reasons, quite apart from reduction of stressful feeling such as tension, anxiety and anger: for stimulation, and a sense of greater energy and vitality; for ritual and the satisfaction of handling the paraphernalia of smoking; for pleasurable relaxation, as after a meal or sex; out of habit or boredom, being almost unaware of taking a cigarette while waiting for someone or something.

The habit may turn into dependence, having to be continued so as to prevent the unpleasant craving which stopping smoking produces.

Attempting to stop smoking is itself a major stress, particularly when physical dependence has developed. Heavy smokers are aware of increase in anger or irritability as they try to stop (and their spouse notices the increased irritability in them for some time). Withdrawal symptoms include restlessness, anxiety, drowsiness, fatigue, insomnia, inability to attend and to concentrate, tremor, palpitations and headache. The craving may go on for weeks or months, and sometimes, though not inevitably, one cigarette can induce total relapse.

how to stop smoking

Giving up smoking is something you cannot do unless you really want to. Saying "I suppose I ought to try and give it up" is not enough. You must feel really positive about it.

A good first step is to think of all the reasons why you would be better off if you did not smoke. Some are only too obvious – for instance, if you have developed a smoker's cough or chronic bronchitis. When reading warnings that smoking can damage your health, lung cancer immediately springs to mind – but the risk of a heart attack from cigarette smoking is even greater than the risk of lung cancer.

Quite apart from damage to health, there is the question of appearance. Smoking a cigarette is no longer the symbol of cool sophistication that it once used to be and, particularly in a heavy smoker, people are more likely to notice the unattractive debris, the stained fingers, and the pervasive smell of tobacco in the room, on your breath, clothes and hair. The smoker may not be aware of this but it could well prove a turn-off for other people.

Do not forget the cost: even for someone who has all the money he needs, it seems a pity to send it up in smoke.

If you cannot stop altogether, cut down as much as possible – to five or less a day. Try not to inhale, and leave a one-third long stub.

People who smoke for stimulation use cigarettes as a means to wake themselves up and to keep going. If this applies to you, you could try taking a brisk walk or moderate exercise instead, breathing slowly and deeply, or taking a mildly stimulating drink such as tea or coffee.

If you smoke to reduce tension, try to divert your tension by some activity: chewing gum or liquorice, sucking a mint, eating fruit or nibbling (a low calorie food); also – depending on where you happen to be at the time – splashing cold water on your face, neck and arms; practising relaxation (yoga or keep-fit classes could help), breathing deeply.

All smokers who are trying to stop should teach themselves a simple form of relaxation to use when they feel tense, or baldy in want of a cigarette.

If you smoke mainly for pleasure, you will need to find some alternative source of satisfaction. Change your pattern of activity, particularly after meals and in tea (or coffee) breaks.

Pleasure from smoking can turn into a craving for tobacco. This can reach the point where putting out one cigarette triggers off the desire for the next one. If you are in this situation, you cannot hope to give up gradually – nothing short of a clean break will work.

A smoker who feels the need to put something into his mouth could try a dummy cigarette. There are lozenges and chewing gum which make cigarettes taste awful, and filters to put into a cigarette holder, designed to remove some of the tar and nicotine, to help to break the smoker's dependence.

Some addicts have stopped smoking by developing an aversion to it through chain smoking non-stop for two days, or until they could not bear the thought of another cigarette – and then stopping, never to smoke again. But this can be a dangerous method: do not try it without consulting your doctor first.

Be sure to choose a good day on which to start the campaign – not when you are under stress. This could be when you are away on holiday or at the start of the weekend, but if you tend to smoke more when you are relaxing and enjoying yourself, stop on a monday morning. If you have 'flu or some other illness during which you are unable to smoke, do not go back to it afterwards.

Ø **Action on Smoking and Health (ASH)**, 5–11 Mortimer Street, London W1N 7RH (telephone 01-637 9843) issues free pamphlets about giving up smoking.

Ø **National Society of Non-Smokers**, 40–48 Hanson Street, London W1P 7DE (telephone 01-636 9103) operates a walk-in information and advice centre and organises regular smoking cessation courses.

Local health education officers can guide people to smoking withdrawal clinics in their area.

A report on smoking, called "No smoking please" was published in *Which?* March 1986.

change in sleeping pattern

Few individuals are capable of switching their problems off when they go to bed. It becomes increasingly difficult to fall asleep, and sleep is unsatisfying and disturbed, with vivid, bad dreams. Insomnia is a common sign of stress.

General tension and tiredness may be the cardinal signs of stress in some people. They find themselves increasingly unable to relax, being on tenterhooks all the time and unable to shut problems out of their mind. The general tension may become so great that the person feels permanently tired, sometimes demanding sleeping pills from the doctor. Eventually there is loss of interest, loss of concentration and loss of memory, making the person seem absentminded and inefficient. Interest in sex diminishes.

Mental stress or pressure is exhausting and can cause a weariness which people misinterpret as physical fatigue; boredom, conflict, tension and anxiety, too, may cause a feeling of weariness. After a stressful day at a desk or counter or workbench, in which physical activity and expenditure of energy has been insignificant, a good long walk may well be more therapeutic than collapsing into an armchair and sitting down all evening, or demanding sleeping pills.

increased drinking, and alcohol dependence

Some people drink for enjoyment or to be sociable; others – clearly stress-related drinkers – in order to allay anxieties and depression. Alcohol is, however, a depressant not a stimulant. Its immediate effect is to remove inhibitions and, in small doses, it can help you to relax, and to lessen anxieties and fears. A small amount facilitates social gatherings, makes the introvert person more extrovert, and makes people more assertive, self-assured and aggressive.

Drinking more can be a sign of increased stress. Someone who normally takes alcohol only in the evening may start drinking at lunch time (perhaps too much, and at the expense of the afternoon's work) to alleviate stress responses. Then he starts drinking whenever a potentially stressful situation looms, so that a bottle may be kept at work and is resorted to increasingly frequently. On return home, the stressed person straight away reaches for a drink and is irritable and uncommunicative until the effects of this drink begin to dissolve the day's stresses.

Job stress, or lack of a job, is clearly identified as one of the main causes for men drinking; women are more likely to drink because of stress in relationships.

Whether a person will drink in a particular situation, and how much, is determined by a number of factors, including how stressed the person feels at the time. There is no such thing as a clearly-defined alcoholic personality. What leads a social drinker to lose control and become a problem drinker or an alcoholic varies from person to person. Family factors are important; occupation affects the likelihood of alcoholism – publicans, actors, seamen and doctors have a high death rate from cirrhosis of the liver.

The alcoholic may drink as a response to stress but his state of dependence is itself a major stress, creating a vicious circle. As a person become psychologically and then bodily dependent on alcohol, the threat or reality of withdrawal symptoms complicates the picture. Withdrawal symptoms include shakiness, sweating, anxiety and depression.

Another side to alcohol dependence is the effect on the person's family. Living with, or being close to, a problem drinker can be very stressful.

Ø **Alcohol Concern**, 305 Grays Inn Road, London, WC1X 8QS (telephone 01-833 3471) is a national charity with three main aims: to raise public awareness of the problems alcohol can cause, to try to improve services for people who are drinking too much and to promote preventive action at a local and national level. The organisation publishes leaflets, booklets and information packs.

Ø **Alcoholics Anonymous**, PO Box 1, Stonebow House, Stonebow, York YO1 2NJ (telephone 0904-644026) is a voluntary worldwide fellowship of people whose joint aim, mutually reinforced, is to attain and maintain sobriety. There are no fees, the only requirement for membership is a desire to stop drinking. The programme is one of total abstinence, based on staying away from one drink one day at a time. In the UK, over 2,300 group meetings are held every week. AA telephone numbers are given in local telephone directories and can often be found in the 'useful numbers' section.

Ø **Al-Anon Family Groups UK and Eire**, 61 Great Dover Street, London SE1 4YF (telephone 01-403 0888 with a 24-hour confidential countrywide service), is a worldwide fellowship providing understanding and support for relatives and close friends of problem drinkers, whether the alcoholic is still drinking or not. There are nearly 1,000 groups in the UK and Eire. For details of your nearest group write or telephone the headquarters. The organisation publishes a number of books, leaflets and other literature.

Ø **Alateen** is a part of Al-Anon especially for young people who are, or have been, affected by an alcoholic relative or close friend. For details of your nearest group, contact Al-Anon.

Ø **Accept** (the name stands for Addictions Community Centres for Education, Prevention, Treatment and Research) Accept Clinic, 200 Seagrave Road, London SW6 1RQ (telephone

01-381 3155) provides team community services and treatment centres for problem and dependent drinkers and their families. Treatment is free and confidential. Accept Studies Centre conducts a range of courses, workshops and seminars. Write or phone (telephone 01-381 2112) for information. The *Drinkwatchers handbook* containing complete information and guidelines on sensible drinking and self-help programmes is available for £2.25 from ACCEPT Publications. **National Drinkwatchers Network** groups and clubs are being established throughout the country for mild problem drinkers and to educate the public in sensible drinking habits.

LIFE EVENTS

In the late 1960s, research conducted in the USA by Dr Thomas Holmes and Dr Richard Rahe led to the publication in the *Journal of Psychosomatic Research* of the 'social readjustment rating scale' – what has become known as the stress chart.

In the British Medical Association's family doctor booklet *Coping with Stress*, these stress ratings, based on Holmes and Rahe, are divided into highest, high, moderate, low, lowest as follows:

EVENTS	STRESS RATING
Death of spouse	**Highest**
Divorce	
Marital separation	
Jail term	
Death of close family member	
Personal injury or illness	
Marriage	
Loss of job	

EVENTS	STRESS RATING
Marital reconciliation	**High**
Retirement	
Change in health of family member	*+ continuing illness*
Pregnancy	
Sex difficulties	
Gain of new family member	*←*
Business readjustment	
Change of financial state	*— Money worries.*
Death of close friend	*Poverty.*

EVENTS	STRESS RATING
Change in number of arguments with spouse	**Moderate**
Large mortgage	
Foreclosure of mortgage or loan	
Change in responsibilities at work	
Son or daughter leaving home	
Trouble with in-laws	
Outstanding personal achievement	

Being at home alone with young children

EVENTS	STRESS RATING
Wife begins or stops work	**Moderate**
Begin or end of school	
Change in living conditions	_— Poor Housing_
Revision of personal habits	
Trouble with boss	

Change in work hours or conditions	**Low**
Change in residence	
Change in schools	
Change in recreation	_Failure to live_
Change in curch/social activities	_up to unrealistic_
Low mortgage or loan	_targets_
Change in sleeping habits	
Change in number of family gatherings	
Change in eating habits	
Vacation	
Christmas	

Minor violations of the law	**Lowest**

The eight 'highest' stress rating situations include death, illness and injury, marriage, divorce and separation – with all of these, the majority of people are familiar, and most people are aware of job loss or the threat of it. Not so with the fourth highest stress event, jail term.

— Caught between conflicting loyalties especially difficult for conscientious people.

ILLNESS AND DEATH

Illness is a major source of stress. This is hardly surprising in view of the major consequences of many illnesses and the fatal nature of some. Worrying about illness is also a source of stress. However, many people have exaggerated fears about their illnesses because they do not know much about medical matters and are reluctant to question their doctors, or when they do ask are given an inadequate explanation or one they do not understand. You may have to persist in questioning. If you do not understand the answers, ask again, perhaps later, particularly if your mind refuses to take in what is being said. It may be useful to have somebody with you as an extra pair of ears.

handicapping illness

Some illnesses lead to permanent handicap such as blindness, deafness, being crippled. If the condition is slowly progressive, the person can adapt to some extent, so that it may not be as stressful as the sudden onset of a handicap.

A chronic illness, or the residual problems following an acute illness, may lead to major financial, social and personal consequences: inability to work can transform a family's circumstances for the worse. Severe stresses can be placed on a marriage, especially when the handicap is disabling. A balance has to be found between over-protecting the invalid who may find dependence on others an added stress (or become over-demanding), and risking extra dangers. Simple things, such as inability to take a holiday, may assume major stressful proportions. Sex may be difficult and a couple should not be too inhibited to seek advice over this.

After the acute phase of a heart attack or stroke, the person is generally left with some disabilities, both physical and psychological. The attack is usually sudden, so there is no chance to acclimatise gradually to the idea of impaired health. Instead, a hitherto healthy person finds his life at some risk and is reminded that he, too, is mortal. Some people who find it difficult to come to terms with this realisation develop a fear of heart attack, believing that any exertion will harm them, and so become invalids unnecessarily.

facing death

Potentially fatal illnesses are particularly stressful not only because of the prospect of pain or of failing bodily functions, but because of fear of the unknown, the unspeakable.

Medical or nursing treatment in which pain is not alleviated adds to stress. The severity of the pain tends to diminish when there is less anxiety about the pain itself. Most people are more stressed when in pain; patients with a terminal illness who are given adequate pain killing drugs are less anxious and distressed. So neither doctor nor patient should underestimate the help that pain killing drugs can give.

The realisation of one's own approaching death is inevitably stressful. Fear, sadness, guilt, anger, regret, disappointment and other emotions may have to be come to terms with. It can be better to express rather than to deny these feelings, and to ask for help in coping with them. At this stage, the best confidant may or may not be a person who is close; possibly a more detached, friendly outsider is more able to accept the validity of what you are saying and feeling, and will not simply set out to cheer you up.

Family and friends of a very ill person are under stress, too, particularly as they cannot offload their worries onto the sick person. They, too, may have to cope with feelings of anger, guilt, sadness, helplessness (which they should try not to abate by undue fussing).

A dying person should not be allowed to be lonely, but that does not mean that the living should spend weeks or months wearing themselves out in constant vigil so that they would have no strength left to cope when necessary. They should try to stay physically and emotionally as fit as possible and ready to offer comfort (if needed). The more attuned they can be to the emotional needs of the person who is facing death, the easier for all concerned. This is not the moment to try to make up for a life-time of discord.

bereavement and grief

The reaction of people to the loss of husband or wife or other close companion varies according to the circumstances and the personalities concerned. Where death has been long foreseen, perhaps after a long or difficult illness, the reaction may be accompanied by relief. This is quite normal. Where the loss is sudden and unexpected, the survivor is overwhelmed, stunned and helpless. The ability to withstand this stressful situation depends in large measure on the support given by others, and the degree to which grief and anguish can be freely expressed during the early stages.

The bereaved person has to come to terms with, and accept the reality of, the death. There are distinct stages in the normal reaction to grief. The first is numbness and disbelief, with automatic and dreamlike behaviour. This stage is usually brief and may last only a day or so; in some rare cases, however, it will extend indefinitely. Then follows a period of prolonged depression, with painful longing for the person who has died and a desire to search for him or her, sometimes accompanied by the feeling that he or she is alive and near. Other people may think this is the beginning of madness; usually these feelings become less intense after a week or two.

This is often followed by a time in which the past relationship is reviewed, blame apportioned for the death and perhaps responsibility laid on doctor, nurses or God. Or the survivor sinks into a state of self-reproach, often about trivial matters. This stage can go on for up to a year, but with diminishing intensity. There is then gradual recovery, shown by improvement in sleep and appetite and a willingness to start new relationships. Grief is probably never completely extinguished but is no longer a constant preoccupation.

expressing grief
Grief is likely to be prolonged if attempts are made to suppress feelings, particularly at the beginning, by self-imposed strictures not to give way.

It is important that the bereaved person should express his or her grief freely in the early stages, and should realise that any mourning process includes feelings of anger as well as sadness. A doctor's help might be sought: sleeping pills or tranquillisers prescribed by the doctor for a short time only can play a part in helping the bereaved and in minimising the immediate stress, especially after a sudden or particularly tragic bereavement.

The help of friends or relatives and neighbours with practical matters (funeral arrangements, financial support, care of children, notifications, clearing up) is also of paramount importance.

Ø **Cruse, Bereavement Care**, 126 Sheen Road, Richmond, Surrey TW9 1UR (telephone 01-940 4818) has branches throughout the country providing a service of counselling to widows and widowers and all bereaved people, practical advice and opportunities for social contact. Where there is no local branch, there is the option of national membership with contact by letter or telephone.

Ø **The Compassionate Friends**, 6 Denmark Street, Bristol, BS1 5DQ (telephone 0272-292778) is an organisation of bereaved parents who seek to help other bereaved parents by giving them the opportunity to talk freely to an understanding and compassionate friend. The organisation has local branches.

Ø **National Associaton of Widows**, Neville House, 14 Waterloo Street, Birmingham, B2 5TX (telephone 021-643 8348) offers information, advice and friendly support to widows and to all those concerned to help widows overcome the many problems they face in society today. Branches throughout the country provide the basis of a supportive social life for widows. A specialist advice and information service is available from the head office. The Association organises regular training seminars and workshops for volunteers and produces a range of leaflets.

About 20 Widows Advisory Centres attached to and manned by volunteers from branches of the National Association of Widows offer advice on all practical and emotional problems faced by widows.

counselling visits
Bereavement counselling is available in some parts of the country, usually provided by voluntary associations that work alongside the local authority services. People are visited in their own home, usually once a week, for a month or two, or longer if necessary. Referrals are made by the doctor, health visitor, social service worker; people can also get in touch with the service direct. A notice about the service may be displayed in local libraries, surgeries and citizens advice bureaux.

STRESS IN MARRIAGE

Getting married, staying married or staying together within a permanent relationship, and the break-up of a marriage or relationship all bring their own stresses. Change, or the threat of change, causes some degree of stress; new and demanding circumstances raise the level of anxiety.

Marriage often has to meet high expectations and to live up to the ideals of romantic love in a social climate in which people have great freedom of choice about how they conduct their lives, and the amount of togetherness or separateness they maintain. After being a protected member inside a family, or being single with perhaps only oneself to please, a series of adaptations will be required. In the past, when marriages were more difficult to dissolve, the legal and domestic framework supported the partners while they made their adjustments, with varying degrees of ease or success.

A strong supportive relationship is important in managing emotional stress and helps people through periods of adjustment. For many people, marriage is the most significant of confiding and supportive relationships.

The framework which a stable relationship provides can support people when they are faced with critical events in their lives. Even an unstable marriage provides a domestic framework.

choice of partner

People seem to choose their partners for unconscious, as well as conscious, reasons. Some people look for a partner who will complement them so that their 'other half' can be, and can do, what they cannot be or do themselves. This can work well provided that the difference is appreciated rather than resented. Taken to excess, it can lead to grim conflict.

Other marriages or relationships are based on identification, a wish for a likeness, even a submission, to the other personality. Stress is caused when it is reluctantly discovered that the partner is a separate and different person who sometimes reacts opposingly to the same event.

People are usually at their most critical when the faults in their partner reflect something in themselves which they cannot handle and do not wish to know about. There is no such thing, outside the realm of imagination, as a marriage free from conflict. If conflict and the stress that derives from it can be seen in a positive light, they can provide the impetus to change and to becoming more mature.

For many people, the idea of marriage or a stable relationship is initially very idealised, invested with hope for what has not been realised before. This is particularly so for people who marry because of an inability to manage a life on their own, or who use marriage as an escape-hatch from an unhappy home, perhaps with their parents.

the roles
The traditional roles of the man and the woman in marriage are considerably less well-defined than in previous generations. An increasing proportion of women go out to work, usually before and after bringing up their children. The woman's continuing wage-earning means that she is not financially dependent on the man. The man who is made aware of the potential redundancy of his role as financial supporter may be stressed by this. The woman may feel trapped by her biological role and feel that she is not fulfilling her potential as a mother if she does not have children, or her potential in the workplace when she does have them.

One cause of stress in marriage today is the envy, often unconscious, of the opposite sex; women envy the still greater opportunities open to men in their careers; men envy the fact that it is still only the women who can bear the children and who can stay home to look after them.

Work interests may clash; the man may expect his wife to

subordinate her career prospects to his, or his frequent changes of location may disrupt her career. Her resentment can produce marital friction and stress. Where a woman outshines the husband professionally, he may feel threatened and be under stress and the marriage suffers.

sex

Sexual difficulties or specific incompatibilities are a common source of stress. Frequency and type of sexual intercourse should ideally be by mutual consent, but this may be difficult to attain. One partner may impose his or her wish for more or less frequent intercourse or may demand practices distasteful to the other. Where such lack of mutual adjustment remains an unspoken problem, it can constitute a nagging stress. Over-emphasis on the sexual aspects of marriage or unreal expectations in one or other partner can lead to unnecessary dissatisfaction and stress. Becoming aware of one's own true reactions and being able to talk to the partner about sexual problems may be the first step towards solving them.

When stress leads to impotence or premature ejaculation in the man, or frigidity in the woman and reluctance to have sex, this leads to further tension within the relationship. Help is available for persistent problems and should be sought before matters become too serious. There are sexual dysfunction clinics or psychosexual clinics in several large hospitals and in some marriage guidance centres, and in some family planning clinics within the NHS (no need for a GP's referral: you can go direct). Some general practitioners offer psychosexual counselling.

Marital infidelities are a well-known stress in marriage, and they may reflect the stresses existing in the marriage as well as causing new ones. Extramarital sex can also cause severe stress when it takes place in unfamiliar, perhaps uncomfortable, surroundings where the couple feel insecure (a heart attack could even result). Sometimes an extramarital affair of which evidence is left lying about can be a symptom of dissatisfaction and an unspoken request for the partner to help in doing something about the stultification of the relationship. The stress caused may lead to a permanent separation or, when the shock has worn off, it may open the way to a more satisfactory marriage.

having children

Children cause stress as well as delight. Childless couples may seem to get more companionship out of their relationship, and many people with children say that their marital satisfaction was highest before they had children.

Through effective contraception, women can decide not to have children. Freedom to make the decision is not, however, necessarily comfortable: the responsibility is in itself a cause of stress. The process of choosing can arouse conflict between partners. The decision whether or not to have children is rarely made on a wholly rational basis.

The prospect of a first child may mean delight for one person, a source of anxiety for another. For most people, it will mean both things and there will be conflicting feelings. While there is joy in a first baby, there is also loss of freedom, for some women the temporary or permanent loss of a job or a career; for both husband and wife, the loss of neat pairing.

There has to be further adaptation from twosome to three-some – and moresome for second and third children. Then there are changing parental roles when these children start school, then leave school; and when 'the nest is emptied' there has to be adaptation back to a twosome.

The needs of children and the demands of careers can be in prolonged conflict. A woman at work during the day is apt to feel resentful that she then has to do the housework, cook and put the children to bed. There are still too few men who share the domestic chores to any appreciable extent, many clinging to their traditional role. The financial sacrifices in having children are often underestimated, especially where the mother takes several years out of her career for her child bearing.

Ø **Exploring Parenthood**, 41 North Road, London, N7 9DP (telephone 01-607 9647) runs workshops at which parents can discuss their problems informally in groups. The workshops are led by a team of qualified professionals drawn from the health service and the social services. All aspects of family life which result in stress are addressed: stress with children of all ages, with partners; stress from conflicts and demands, from financial and unemployment worries; single parenthood, step-parenting, mixed marriages, handicapped children and parents, fostering and adoption.

Workshops are held regularly in central London and throughout the country at the request of any parent or professional group.

quarrelling and conflict

Emotions operate intensely in marriage, as they do in any close relationship and, inevitably, lead to some measure of conflict, frustration and aggressive reaction against the partner.

'A quarrel a day keeps divorce away' may not be everybody's ideal of marital satisfaction, but arguments and even quarrels are not necessarily destructive if the dissatisfaction, frustration, conflicts, even fury, can be expressed in words and people are willing to listen to each other.

However distressing arguments and quarrels may be, they at least release tension. Continuously repressed feelings which fester can give rise to physical and psychiatric symptoms such as extreme tiredness and depression.

If the argument, although heated, is always related to trivialities or a particular triviality, this may mean that the quarrel is really about something more fundamental and help may be needed to understand the underlying meaning. Try to analyse your last quarrel: was your anger directed at the right person (difficulties at work, or a long-hidden conflict with a parent, taken out on the husband?); were you arguing about the right thing (ostensibly about the washing up, but perhaps really about who neglected whom over the past few weeks?); was the timing an aggravating factor (when the in-laws were coming to visit?); did it reveal past grievances that you thought long dead and forgotten (harbouring grudges leads to stress).

The first step is resolving any conflict is to decide what the conflict is really about. Often, a surface issue is only a symbol of an underlying more crucial conflict. Thus, not being able to decide with your spouse where to go for a holiday, although a minor problem in itself, may reflect a conflict over who makes major decisions and how.

If you keep on having disagreements about the same sort of thing, identifying the recurring theme may reveal the real conflict associated with it. Learning to identify the causes of conflict requires practice. The types of issue that often lie at the bottom of conflicts are

○ conflict over roles (for example, if a wife wants a husband to share in the domestic chores but he thinks this violates his concept of masculinity)
○ conflict over values (for example, whether to follow an altruistic but ill-paid career as against a lucrative but socially dubious one)
○ conflict over spending and saving
○ conflict over who gets their way (for instance, if one person always chooses the TV programme despite the protests of the rest of the family)
○ conflict over being right on factual matters (some people are both opinionated and reluctant to put their facts to the test).

Being over-assertive can also give rise to conflict. Standing up for one's rights may be useful when dealing with bureaucracy but is a recipe for disaster in family discussion. Winning an argument may alienate the rest of the family; it may be better to concede a point in order to set up favourable conditions for the resolution of other conflicts. The art of compromise needs to be learned by many people who take into marital and family life the uncompromising attitudes and stances which they believe necessary at work.

If hostility continues despite seemingly solving the apparent conflict, deeper issues will need to be brought into the open and resolved.

seeking help

It is important that a couple who have a marital problem seek help sooner rather than later – before bitterness and hurt drive them further apart.

Inherent in the process of seeking help must be the wish for change: in oneself as well as in the partner. Counselling that is used as a forum for blame will prove ineffective. The prospect of change in oneself, however, is frightening and this in itself raises anxiety because change is a step into the unknown.

A counsellor is trained to help people to talk about their marital problems so that they will see their difficulties in a clearer perspective and consider the possible courses of action open to them. Counselling may, therefore, be a lengthy process, taking several interviews. Application to a marriage guidance council can be made jointly by a couple, or individually by either husband or wife. Counselling can be successful without the other spouse attending as well.

The work with a marriage guidance counsellor – and it can be hard work – may lead to a more satisfying marriage. Or it may lead to a positive or less destructive separation. The aim of marriage counselling is not to save marriages at all costs; there is more concern about emotional growth and development of insight so that even if a marriage has to end, the same type of mistake need not be made a second time.

Ø The headquarters of various marriage guidance or advisory councils are RELATE, **National Marriage Guidance Council**,

Herbert Gray College, Little Church Street, Rugby, CV21 3AP (telephone 0788-73241); **Scottish Marriage Guidance Council**, 26 Frederick Street, Edinburgh, EH2 2JR (telephone 031-225 5006); **Catholic Marriage Advisory Council**, Clitherow House, 1 Blythe Mews, Blythe Road, London, W14 0NW (telephone 01-371 1341); **Jewish Marriage Council**, 23 Ravenhurst Avenue, London, NW4 4EL (telephone 01-203 6311).

Interviews are by appointment, mostly made by telephone, or by personal application to the larger offices. A first appointment might be offered within a few days, but in some places it may be a few weeks. Interviews last up to an hour; they are generally weekly.

For many people it is not easy to approach a counselling body; it seems an admission of failure and unhappiness.

Ø **The Institute of Marital Studies**, Tavistock Centre, 120 Belsize Lane, London, NW3 5BA (telephone 01-435 7111) is a centre of advanced study and practice in marital work and offers a therapeutic service. Both partners are asked to attend for regular weekly therapy sessions, and may be seen together or separately according to their needs and circumstances. A consultation and referral service is also offered to individuals whose partner is unable or unwilling to attend for therapy. Fees for the service are negotiated according to the financial circumstances of those in receipt of help.

Marriage has never been more open to question, and yet more people are married than ever before, many people divorce in order to marry again, and the expectations placed on marriage appear to remain as strong as ever – and so does the need for affection, humour, loyalty, kindness, tolerance, support.

aggression in the family

People under stress become short-tempered and irritable, resenting questions, snapping back. Hostility is sometimes not shown towards the person at the root of the problem but as displaced aggression towards someone else, who becomes the scapegoat. This is likely to happen if the source of stress is a person in a position of power or superiority, such as one's parents or boss.

Aggression can take a physical form. Wife-battering is a form of assault resulting from aggressive impulses. It has a long history and is still regarded by some men as acceptable behaviour and by some women as a fact of life. Sometimes, the aggression is a form of sexual release or precedes sexual intercourse. In other cases, the aggression stems from stress or provocation. The frustrations of unemployment, straightened circumstances, unwanted children, lead to venting aggression on the partner.

Baby battering is not a new phenomenon; doctors are alerted to the fact that unusual or repeated injuries in babies and children may not be accidental. The parents may themselves be perpetuating a cycle, reacting to stress and problems with physical aggression.

Parents may find themselves becoming increasingly irritable and snappy because of tiredness and shortness of sleep. They should try to take turns at minding the baby or child, and should try to agree between themselves on what line to take with the child, so as not to add to the stress by additional discord.

The support of one's family and friends should not be underestimated. It is worth trying to keep lines of communication open with family and friends who often do not approach for fear of being rebuffed for interfering – try to make use of the informal family/friend network for sharing and unburdening problems.

Ø **Women's Aid Federation (England) Ltd**, PO Box 391, Bristol BS99 7WS (telephone 0272 420611) is the national office for women's refuges which provide temporary accommodation to women and their children who are suffering physical, mental or sexual abuse.

Women suffering domestic violence who need advice, information or emergency refuge should telephone 0272 428368.

For Scotland and Wales, national offices are **Scottish Women's Aid**, 11 St. Colme Street, Edinburgh EH3 6AG (24 hour telephone 031 255 8011), **Welsh Women's Aid**, 38–48 Crwys Road, Cardiff CF2 4NN (telephone 0222 390874) and 9 Castle Street, Aberystwyth, Dyfed, SY23 1DT (telephone 0970 612748, staffed by Welsh speakers). The contact for Northern Ireland is **Northern Ireland Women's Aid**, 143a University Street, Belfast BT7 1HP (telephone 0232 249041 or 249348).

Ø **Parents Anonymous (London)**, 6 Manor Gardens, London N7 6LA (telephone 01-263 8918), has parent volunteers who provide a telephone helpline, offering a listening ear to parents in distress, who either have abused, or feel they may abuse, their children. Similar groups exist elsewhere sometimes under names such as **Parent lifeline** or **Families under stress**.

Ø **Organisations for Parents under Stress**, 106 Godstone Road, Whyteleafe, Surrey, CR3 0EB (telephone 01-645 0469) is a co-ordinating body under the umbrella name OPUS that can give parents the phone number of a group in their part of the country.

If there are organised groups in the community – mother and toddler groups, young wives', church, drop-in centres, self-help groups, places where you find others with similar difficulties – take advantage of them; it helps to know that you are not the only one.

stress in childhood

Even for young children, life can contain stressful experiences; but where the child is surrounded by love and security such experiences are very unlikely to have lasting effects. Moreover, the successful negotiation of mild stress in early life can provide a valuable foundation for adequate coping later.

Coping with stress is learned from childhood onwards – and parents can help to teach children how to cope. By putting her arms around a distressed child, a mother does more good than by shouting and scolding, as often happens. People who have not been treated in an understanding manner by their parents will not find it easy to be understanding parents when they themselves have children.

It is important for adults to be aware of some regularly occurring events in the lives of most children which can be experienced by some of them as sources of considerable stress.

A small child has to contend with things such as being restrained and chastised, fear of the dark, being left alone, teasing, not being given things, having to share, the arrival of a new baby.

the birth of a new baby

The arrival of a new sister or brother is almost always a happy occasion for children as well as parents. It is important, however, to keep existing children as fully informed as possible about the impending event and to involve them in looking forward to, and preparing for, the birth. Introducing the topic should be a fairly matter-of-fact part of conversation by the time the pregnancy is physically obvious.

The new baby will be the centre of attraction, once it arrives. If other young members of the family are to share fully and joyfully in this experience, it is important they they too should enjoy a little extra attention at this time. This can be especially important for the displaced baby of the family, particularly at the birth of a second child.

Sensitivity to the feelings of the existing children goes a long way towards providing them with the reassurance that, although they may no longer be quite the centre of attention that they once were, their parents' love for them remains secure and undiminished.

school

Entry into kindergarten, playgroup or school is exciting and challenging; new experiences are confronted, new friendships are formed. For many children, this is the first experience of being away from home, being away from the primary caretaker for any length of time. For children who stand secure in their attachment with their parents, these minor separations will be negotiated without difficulty, even though some youngsters will initially need more reassurance. Where, however, a child shows persistent, inconsolable separation anxiety, this may be a signal that the youngster is experiencing insecurity in relationships with the parents and it may be worthwhile seeking professional advice, for example through your GP or local child guidance service.

Change of school, from infant to primary to secondary, can mean change of environment, change of teachers, change of discipline, change of friends as well as change of curriculum. All these changes require adjustment and make demands on the child. Most children accommodate to these demands fairly readily, but parents should be aware that temporary arrest in scholastic progress is widespread at times of change of school and that their children need understanding and reassurance rather than criticism at such times.

school problems

Unhappiness at school can be caused by a host of factors – failure to live up to parental expectation, especially if the parents consider the child's lack of achievement at school to be due to lack of ambition or application. Nowadays even the least able will be expected to become computer-literate to some extent, and even a dull child cannot escape without pressure. At the other extreme, being a gifted or precocious child can also be stressful because of the expectations aroused in adults, and feeling the odd-one-out amongst other children.

There may also be dislike by, or of, particular teachers, peer group pressure or even bullying or scapegoating by other children. Sympathetic, sensitive cooperation between parent, school and child is needed to resolve the majority of such difficulties. Warning bells should start ringing, however, where children truant or where they regularly complain of symptoms of illness at times when they should be preparing to go to school, or show other forms of school phobia. As with separation anxiety in earlier childhood, these can be symptoms of basic insecurity in the child's emotional life. Again, it may be worth seeking professional assistance.

Exams, including the build-up beforehand and the anxiety afterwards, obviously constitute a great stress. One practical way of helping is not to add to the stress by making too light of the problem or by nagging. This is not the time for sudden bouts of discipline; rather the youngster should be protected from family encroachment, including that of brothers and sisters.

a mind of one's own – adolescence

One of the great psychological discoveries which young people make in the course of growing up is that their own minds can be a source of knowledge. They realise that it is possible to think things out for themselves, that they can create new solutions to old problems, that conventions are just that – conventions – and that things need not be the way they are. It is a process that begins around early adolescence and for many young people this is an exciting, even heady time. Authority begins to be challenged and young people are no longer satisfied with "Because I say so" or "Because that's the way it is" exhortations for compliance. They want to know "Why?" and to share in negotiation over rules and standards.

The adolescent wants emotional and intellectual independence from his parents but is still tied in many overt and subtle ways. It is a time of swings between wanting to be an adult and free, and wanting to be a child and protected, a time of critically challenging parental values. The stress on the parents lies in having to re-examine their values in the face of sometimes very unsubtle criticism.

The accelerating growth of independence can be stressful for young people and for their parents. For the young people, the stress arises from the conflict between the need to assert themselves and the need to avoid isolating themselves from their primary sources of emotional support – the parents. For parents, stress can arise from the challenge to their own egos which may result from their children's assertiveness; authoritative individuals in particular may find this a difficult experience to cope with.

The physical changes of maturation also have to be coped with. Relationships, particularly sexual and emotional ones with other adolescents, are often tentative or unstable and can be a particular source of stress, though not necessarily a bad stress. There may be doubts over sexual orientation or misgivings over sexual attractiveness; whether or not to become sexually active preoccupies many teenagers. Lots of adolescents are frightened of sex, to which is added the fear of AIDS.

In a very few teenagers, problems and anxieties can show themselves in behavioural disturbances such as vandalism, gang-fights, truancy, shop-lifting expeditions, risking a brush with the law. This may be revolt, or a reaction to boredom, on the part of the children. Most adolescents tend to take life quite seriously and are very law-abiding, but one problem is that there is nowhere for kids to go. Church socials do not appeal to many, cinemas have closed down, discos are expensive and, anyway, discos are thought by some adults to be 'where drinking, sex and drugs go on' – and adolescents like to perpetuate the myth. The parents have to find a middle way between open anger or shock and apparent apathy, and should show that they care, without actively interfering. What they should try not to do is relieve their own stresses at the expense of their children.

If there has been 'glasnost' – openness – in the home from the earlier days of childhood, these stresses will be manageable for parents and children alike; indeed, such openness can be the optimal procedure for reducing the likelihood of these stresses ever arising.

Ø **National Children's Home**, 85 Highbury Park, London N5 1UD (telephone 01-226 2033) is a Christian voluntary organisation working with children, youngsters and young families covering a wide range of needs. It runs family centres, residential centres and schools, alternatives to custody, independence training units, and many specialist community projects. Many of the services involve stress support.

Ø **NCH Careline** is the nationwide telephone counselling service provided by the National Children's Home. Apart from the phone-in facility many Carelines can offer face-to-face counselling and other services. It is able to help with the whole range of problems which affect families and young people. Careline also provides telephone counselling for NCH's Young Runaways project which helps young people who have either left home or are thinking of doing so.

Telephone numbers of countrywide services can be obtained by writing in to the Highbury Park address or (in office hours only) by phoning 01-226 2033. Another telephone number, open from 9 am to 9.30 pm, is 0532 456 456, where the caller will be given the nearest local Careline number (of which there are 15 throughout the country).

Ø **National Association of Young Peoples Counselling and Advisory Services**, 17/23 Albion Street, Leicester LE1 6GD (telephone 0533-558763) is a registered charity which co-ordinates a network of youth counselling and advisory services throughout the country.

NAYPCAS provides advice, support and counselling to member agencies and promotes good practice through its training and publications.

The *Someone To Talk To* directory published by the Mental Health Foundation includes pages of details of counselling services for young people; there is a 'Students Nightline' in many towns and 'Message Home' a 24-hour service for runaway children to leave messages without having to give their whereabouts. The numbers are given in the local telephone directories.

Ø **ChildLine** is the free national helpline for children in trouble or in danger, offering a 24 hour confidential counselling service. Call free on 0800 1111 or write to ChildLine, Freepost 1111, London EC4B 4BB.

family stress

Situations which, combined with other adverse factors, can lead to increase in stress, include:

MARITAL PROBLEMS
lack of communication
differences in interests
financial problems
sexual disappointments/
    incompatibility
very high expectations
differing priorities
different sleeping habits
spouse who snores
spouse who is overweight
jealousy
unfaithfulness
planning holidays with conflicting
    interests
failing to share domestic chores
spouse's smoking and drinking
    habits
lack of compliments
conflicting careers
death of the spouse

SOCIAL PROBLEMS
lack of morality
class discrimination
permissiveness
racial tensions
overcrowding
social isolation
housing shortage
mismatch between eligible men and
    women
violence and hooliganism

CHILDREN PROBLEMS
crying baby
sick child
disobedient children
jealous siblings
expensive toys
not enough time with children
handicapped child
food likes and dislikes
transporting children
conflict between personal and
    children's interests
child who plays truant
poor school performance
lack of respect for parents or teachers
teenagers with untidy rooms
loud music
excessive use of telephone
late night parties
children in trouble with police
teenage pregnancy
changing work ethos of the young
generation gap

OTHER FAMILY PROBLEMS
to marry or not to
single parent family
divorce
ageing parents
demanding in-laws
unplanned pregnancy
to have or not have children
relatives with unreasonable
    expectations
disharmony with neighbours

STRESS IN DIVORCE

The ease of divorce has led to a destabilisation of marriage, and to a growing feeling that a marriage is not necessarily 'for keeps'. Although divorce is relatively simple, repairing a marriage is difficult.

Nevertheless, marriage is more difficult to get out of than to get into, not only legally and materially, but also emotionally. A divorce (other than one which legalises a long-standing separation) is never free from stress, tension, conflict, regret, apprehension, sadness and pain.

During the long drawn-out process of disengagement, the participants fluctuate between hope and despair before one or both partners will finally acknowledge that their marriage is a failure, for which it is no longer worthwhile to make the sacrifice and effort required to maintain it. Separation, even when it is not felt as a supreme tragedy, presents a difficult period of transition from one type of life to another, with all its uncertainties which may continue for many years.

There are obvious differences in the impact on the partner who finds him/herself unloved, rejected, imposed on or only reluctantly agreeing to the divorce and the one who is the prime mover, accepts the responsibility, does the leaving. However, the situation is rarely so unambiguous: the rejected sometimes becomes the rejector, the 'innocent' is beset with guilt. Both partners are likely to feel aggrieved, misused, condemned by the other. The lives of both undergo disruption with regard to children, family, friends; and both have to negotiate a change of social identity quite apart from all the financial implications.

In terms of stress, divorce ranks second only to bereavement in the list of stress chart factors; some people who have experienced both say that being divorced is more desolating than being widowed. Widowhood usually invites an unambiguous sympathy and a degree of support not generally afforded to the divorced; the elements of choice and responsibility, shame, a sense of failure or humiliation, and even of condemnation do not figure in widowhood.

In both situations there is loss. In divorce, there may be loss of sexual intimacy, bodily contact and warmth; loss of a particular lifestyle, perhaps loss of home; for one partner, loss of day-to-day contact with children; and, perhaps most distressing of all, loss of hope and ideals. There is, therefore, much to be mourned, however difficult the preceding circumstances may have been.

a kind of mourning

People appear to make better adjustments to new situations when they can recognise and come to terms with what they have had to give up. Only then, it seems, can they fully appreciate the satisfactions of the altered circumstances.

In any normal mourning process there are certain discernible phases which may overlap. After the first shock and disbelief that 'this could happen to me', there is a phase of acute anxiety and disorientation when the implications of the loss start to make themselves felt. Then, during a phase of yearning and searching for what is lost, many desperate last attempts at reconciliation may be made, despite the realisation of a lost cause. This is followed by a phase of anger, uncomfortably mixed with guilt. Finally, there is a period of emptiness, before hope renews itself and the person can find new meaning in life. The whole process may well take two years after a bereavement – after a divorce, it may take five.

Mourning ceases to be normal when the process is unduly prolonged or stuck in one phase or another; for example, if anger gets more and more vitriolic, or the search for what is lost becomes waiting for a miraculous return, or if the feeling of emptiness intensifies into a full-blown depressive illness.

There is often an amazing sense of continuing attachment and belonging, either to the person whom you want to leave, or to the person who has left you, even when love has died. For some people it seems remarkably tenacious and, even after many years of separation, dormant feelings of attachment to an ex-spouse can be reawakened. This sense of connectedness may prevent people from going through the necessary mourning for what has been lost, and makes it difficult for the abandoned partner not to construe any kind word or considerate action on the part of the ex-partner as a gesture of reconciliation. Even the abandoner, going directly to another potentially permanent mate, may, insteading of finding relief, be unable to shake off feelings of extreme disequilibrium.

mixed feelings

Most people have mixed feelings about divorce and continue to wonder whether they should try harder. But if something is inevitable, it does not help to put it off for too long.

Some people deal with uncertainty by denying its existence and cutting the knot as swiftly and as cleanly as possible, in an urge to get it all over and done with. The speed with which divorces can be obtained is not always helpful: people can find themselves taken over by a legal process which outstrips their emotional capacities while they remain hopelessly entangled and divided in their feelings. In many cases, a divorce can be obtained quite easily 'by post' without involving a solicitor. Where solicitors are consulted, some are attuned to the ambivalence, and recognise the signs when an initial request for legal advice is to be used only as a threat to the marriage partner. They may help by referring the couple to a counselling agency; others are not so perceptive.

The primitive feelings of anger and hurt are sometimes re-directed on to the problems of apportionment of money and property and prolonged disputes over care of and access to children. The problems are real enough and there may be no 'right' answer, but some couples find it difficult to achieve any form of agreement and are unable seriously to consider what would be best for the children; in their bruised and insecure state, they feel more childlike than adult themselves. Sometimes the fight is unconsciously maintained to ward off the grief and emptiness that might follow: a fight is one way of prolonging a relationship.

the children

Children can be seriously affected by continued parental conflict in the home.

When and how to tell the children is a problem for most people, particularly when they have tried to hide the conflict and have not wanted to disturb the children unnecessarily before a firm decision is made. However, children have long antennae and long ears, even when doors are closed, and are uncannily perceptive to atmosphere. Leaving them in the dark when their every sense tells them that their world is about to fall apart, can cause them even greater stress.

The children will inevitably be upset in their own right, suffering their own separation anxiety, and perhaps showing symptoms of quite severe disturbance. Bad behaviour may hide an anxiety about what is going to happen to them in the threatened separation which they may fear is all their fault. It is a tremendous burden for children to carry their parents' marriage if they know that they are the only reason for its maintenance, but most children initially try to get their parents to stay together.

some consequences
Less stressful for the adults are children who develop a precocious maturity, act as conciliators, and end up by parenting their parents. Children who are forced into a false maturity are later likely to show the distress they suffered when the situation is again safe enough for them to do so.

Children are upset and disturbed by their parents' separating and by sometimes radically changed circumstances in their lives. Their school work is likely to deteriorate because they will be less able to concentrate while they are worrying about what is going to happen to them and until they are assured in fact, as well as in words, that they have not lost their parents' love and concern and that they do not miss out too much under the new arrangements. During this period they may be more vulnerable to infections and accidents, and they may become more babyish in their behaviour. All of this is very stressful to an already distressed parent.

the parents' responsibility
Separation from a parent as the consequence of a breakdown of the parental relationship is a traumatic experience for children; their emotional security is threatened and they need to be reassured of the continued, unqualified love of both their parents. Thus, at the time of separation, parents have a responsibility not to create further conflict by requiring the children to take the side of one or another of them. If the parents themselves can handle this without a scene, it is preferable that they should speak to the children together about the separation and about subsequent arrangements for care and access. In these explanations, it is important that the parents should be mutually consistent and should, therefore, be clear themselves what arrangements have been made and how they are to be presented to the children.

Children cope best with the trauma of divorce when the subsequent relationship between the estranged spouses is reasonably amicable, where care and access arrangements are mutually agreed between the former partners and where neither parent seeks to draw the children into a coalition against the other. It is where acrimony and conflict characterise the post-separation relationship between the partners that the experience of divorce is at its most traumatic for children and adults alike.

Children are, however, adaptable creatures and, as their worlds settle down again, they can recover their equilibrium. There may be aspects they dislike and for some time they may be very angry with the missing parent; but some children recover more quickly than the parents, who moreover may have to carry the extra stress of single-parenting.

helping oneself

People can attempt to lern from the experience of those around them in similar circumstances. They will find support when they discover that their fears and feelings are not abnormal and that others have felt likewise. If mourning can be allowed to run its course, and the feelings of loss, anger and guilt are allowed to surface, this helps in the healing process. Thwarted and stored up, these emotions may cause breakdown later, if a second severe loss is experienced. When there is something to grieve for, expressing one's grief is healthy.

professional help
People should not be afraid to seek professional help, if necessary. Friends and relatives may not allow them to show their grief or let them go over and over the whys and where-fores of the breakdown of the marriage. Professional ears are used to such anguish, know what is within the realm of the normal and can lend emotional strength. An hour a week with a psychotherapist, marriage guidance counsellor or social worker may enable a distressed person to get through the rest of the week.

More marital problems are taken to general practitioners than to the specialist agencies; sometimes the problem is presented directly and openly, sometimes through an illness. Some GPs are prepared to listen and even offer a follow-up; most can provide an appropriate referral, if approached.

Marriage guidance agencies offer their services to those who want help in parting (not only to those who want help to stay together) and to those who, caught up in the ambivalence, just do not know what they want.

More and more emphasis is nowadays placed on conciliation, trying to help couples to resolve as many problems as possible by mutual agreement. There are new conciliation services in various parts of the country, some independent and voluntary (sometimes fee-charging), some attached directly to the courts. These services are designed to help couples who have made the decision to divorce but are unable to come to an agreement on their own regarding the care of the children and apportionment of resources. They aim to help people to separate as constructively as possible. Citizens advice bureaux should be able to provide addresses and details.

Ø **National Family Conciliation Council**, 34 Milton Road, Swindon SN1 5JA (telephone 0793-618486) (administrator Mrs Jenny Bassett), has at present about 40 fully affiliated services. The primary aim of conciliation is to help couples involved in the process of separation and divorce to reach agreements, or reduce the area or intensity of conflict between them, especially on disputes concerning their children.

Ø **Gingerbread**, 35 Wellington Street, London WC2E 78N (telephone 01-240 0953) is a nationwide organisation providing support for lone parents and their children. There are self-help groups throughout the country, organising such services as babysitting, crisis support, play schemes and family activities (telephone numbers obtainable by ringing national office). There is a phone-in advice service plus a wide range of publications; list and contacts for local groups are available from the national office.

Ø **National Council for the Divorced and Separated**, contact address the treasurer at 62 Stourview Close, Mistley, Manningtree, Essex CO11 1LZ, has over 100 branches throughout the British Isles which provide a venue where people with similar experiences and problems can meet and make new friends and develop new interests. Most branches have a welfare officer; there is also an individual member scheme.

Ø **The National Council for One Parent Families**, at 255 Kentish Town Road, London NW5 2LX (telephone 01-267 1361) offers help and advice. The service is free and confidential and includes legal advice and help with problems such as housing, social security, taxation and maintenance.

loneliness

Much of the distress caused by any psychological problem stems from worrying about having the problem, as much as from the problem itself. In loneliness (and shyness) much of the distress is the worry about being shy or lonely rather than the loneliness itself. This is all the more so because some people think that being alone is a sign of personal failure, their own fault and unique to them. There is nothing inherently shameful or unnatural about being alone: being alone should not be equated with being a social failure.

There are some characteristics attributed to lonely people – being negative, rejecting, self-absorbed, self-deprecating and unresponsive – but these can all be reversed. Sometimes people need no more than brief social skills therapy in which they acquire some basic linguistic and non-verbal tenets of social intercourse. This may be as simple as saying 'hello, how are you?' and smiling, which they may have failed to learn to do when young. Sometimes counselling is the right solution, sometimes just the opportunity to meet people will relieve the symptoms of stress.

Ø **The National Federation of Solo Clubs**, Rooms 7/8 Ruskin Chambers, 191 Corporation Street, Birmingham B4 6RY (telephone 021-236 2879) is a large voluntary organisation for the lonely, widowed, divorced, separated or single between the ages of 25 and 65. Members are welcomed at any or all of over a hundred clubs throughout the country. There is a hostess to welcome the shy newcomer; a welfare officer will visit sick members and help with problems. The Federation runs a national holiday each year at which members from all parts of the country can come together, and most of the clubs also arrange their own holidays at home and abroad.

Ø **The Outsiders Club**, Box 4ZB, London W1A 4ZB (telephone 01-499 0900) helps people who feel emotionally isolated, perhaps because of their social or physical disabilities, by welcoming them into the club to meet and help each other. There are social activities in London and elsewhere for anyone who wants to come: these are unthreatening events where shy and inexperienced people can feel happy.

Loneliness is found not only among the disabled, the housebound or the elderly, but also among younger people who have been divorced, widowed, or are single parents. Loneliness, being no respector of persons, can hit the occupant of a luxury flat as much as a youngster in a lowly bedsit. People who, for whatever reason, would rather express their thoughts to strangers who live at a distance than to those with whom they live cheek by jowl, can take advantage of

Ø **Conversation by correspondence through friends by post**, 6 Bollin Court, Macclesfield Road, Wilmslow, Chester SK9 2AP (telephone 0625-527004), which is a service for letter exchange between people who have nobody to talk to. Sharing one's daily life problems even in writing can increase interest, release stresses and may help to overcome depression.

assertiveness

The basis of assertive behaviour (which is not the same as aggressiveness) is self-confidence. Assertiveness recognises that it is a basic human right to have respect for oneself and others, expressed by honesty in relationships, by saying yes when you mean yes and no when you mean no. Poor self-assertion is bad for morale and can lead to aggressive behaviour in everyday situations where a person loses control or becomes angry. Alternatively, it is expressed in submissive behaviour where a person says nothing and keeps true feelings hidden.

Both aggressive and submissive behaviour are potential stressors if they become a habitual way of reacting to difficult situations. Both stem from feelings of personal inadequacy and both are response mechanisms to counteract a perceived threat. In the short-term, each produces the feeling that the 'danger' has been coped with. The long-term effect of such inappropriate behaviour is to lose other people's respect and so reinforce low self-esteem.

It is not easy to learn to be assertive and to be straightforward in communicating with others, but it is always worth the effort. Assertion training courses are available, mostly in London, varying from one-day workshops to courses lasting several weeks. You can obtain a list of teachers in your area, both in London and outside, by approaching MIND (22 Harley Street, London W1N 2ED) for a booklist and list of current training courses.

growing older

The middle age of life (which in women includes the menopause) is classically regarded as a time of stress. Having to worry about elderly parents, particularly when they start to be ailing and failing, takes over from worrying about the children. The strain of looking after someone, particularly an elderly parent or infirm relative, on top of carrying on a full time job, can be so stressful that in the end it is the carer who needs emotional and psychological help.

Ø **National Council for Carers and their Elderly Dependents**, 29 Chilworth Mews, London W2 3RG (telephone 01-724 7776) provides a service of information and guidance for people who have, or have had, the care of elderly or infirm dependents at home. There are local branches which provide support and represent the interests of carers with dependents.

Ø **Association of Carers** and the National Council for Carers plan to work as one organisation, from the spring of 1988, under the (provisional) name of Carer's National Association; contact address 29 Chilworth Mews, London W2 3RG.

Ø **Alzheimer's Disease Society**, 158–160 Balham High Street, London SW12 9BN (telephone 01-675 6557), backs a network of support groups offering help to families; publishes a non-clinical manual which explains the various symptoms, and suggests practical ways of handling the disease.

adjusting

Reappraising one's life at mid-point shows up the missed opportunities, with the realisation that what has not yet been achieved may never be. Disappointment at work may become particularly acute and the ensuing frustrations spill over into family life.

When children grow up and leave home, the parents' role changes. A woman who does not go out to work and whose main focus has been the home and the family, will almost certainly have difficulty adjusting to the effects of 'the empty nest' and is likely to show symptoms of stress. The so-called 'mid-life crisis' is a period of readjustment; some people cope less well than others with the stresses that occur. But by middle age, many people have at least learned what they like and do not like, so there is a better change of following one's true inclinations and of building up interests outside work or the immediate family. This may also help towards a less stressful old age.

in old age

Physical illness in old age is a further source of stress, particularly chronic or crippling disease and handicaps. Being housebound can aggravate the situation, and so can awareness of failing mental and physical powers, and the worry about 'being a burden'.

The stresses of old age can be made worse by lack of resources and reserves. Some old people who are now retired feel useless, particularly someone who is now living under more straitened circumstances. Worse, he (or more usually

she) may have lost a spouse. The sense of futility and useless-
ness may depress and stress an old person to the point of
contemplating suicide – even after a full life well spent. Being
made to feel useful and needed can be as important as proper
physical care in old age.

Stress may be mitigated by the old person's long experience
of life: he has seen it all before, and has developed strategies for
dealing with untoward or unusual occurrences. However,
some old people lose their adaptability and their resourcefulness, and personality characteristics become exaggerated, the
old person becoming more suspicious, or more irritable or
more difficult; the younger ones can help by reassurance – and
much patience.

THE WORLD AROUND US

For city dwellers, the sheer numbers of other human beings milling about, queuing up for things, obstructing each other, is a stress. Overcrowding is a known source of stress which has been studied in laboratory animals. A colony of mice will increase in number rapidly but, when a peak is reached, the mouse population is not maintained and actually decreases despite the space being the same and food being freely available. In human societies, population densities above a certain amount are inherently stressful, too, but among humans, who are less sensible than mice, overcrowding continues and increases in cities. In overcrowded and under-priviliged areas there is competition for space, amenities and facilities. The stresses may be partly offset where the pressures have the effect of generating community mutual aid.

noise

Noise is a major source of stress. Inescapable noise, such as traffic noise close to trunk roads and motorways, often reaches intolerable levels and so does aircraft noise for people living under the flight path of busy airports (ear-plugs and double glazing can help). There is also the relentlessness of loud and uncongenial music in shops and pubs – those, however, you can avoid.

Be aware that you too may be adding to somebody else's stress by banging car doors, keeping the car engine running in the early hours, riding a non-suppressed motor-bike, or using a personal stereo turned up so loud as to be no longer 'personal'. Often the person who unwittingly creates noise that is intolerable to others, is unaware of it. If possible, use noisy equipment only when there is no one else around, so as not to push up the general stress levels.

noise from neighbours

If you have noisy neighbours, tell them that they are disturbing you – they may not be aware of it. And tell them what, in particular, is causing trouble: loud music, animals, plumbing. Have an informal discussion with them to see if you can reach an amicable agreement. Remember any noise caused by you yourself might equally disturb them, or others.

If this has no effect, and you still suffer from the noise, three formal courses of action are open to you: complain to the local authority, complain direct to magistrates' court (in Scotland, summary application to the sheriff court), civil action – that is, taking the neighbour to court yourself. However, in taking up any matter which involves a neighbour, bear in mind that you will be living opposite or alongside each other for many years to come, and will want to enjoy a reasonably happy relationship. So, in the first place, try to talk things over and try to sort out problems in an amicable fashion before taking action, and use tact or diplomacy whenever you can.

Mediation centres, a fairly new idea to Britain, offer a counselling service for neighbours in dispute. They aim to solve problems amicably, and without having to go to court. During a session, complaints are aired from both sides and then discussed. A compromise may well be agreed. At present, there are only a handful of mediation centres in Britain. If you have a neighbour dispute, and think your neighbour would be willing to attend a mediation session, contact your local council to find out if there is a centre near you.

driving and traffic

The relentless growth of cities has led to severe transport problems. Buses or taxis, where available, become hopelessly bogged down in traffic jams; commuters increasingly use their cars and the increase in private cars adds to the traffic jams.

It is commonplace in big cities for commuters to drive for an hour or more in the morning and evening rush-hours.

Traffic jams are a prime source of personal frustration and mechanical overheating. Drivers unlucky enough to be stuck in summer snarl-ups should keep themselves and their cars cool. Frustration should never be taken out on other motorists. If the congestion looks like lasting more than a few seconds, switch off the engine.

Driving in heavy traffic has been shown to be a powerful stress, with rapid and extreme rises in heart rate and blood pressure.

The stress in driving comes from the accumulation of a number of factors – traffic, weather conditions, getting lost, trouble with the car, noise and vibration, passengers, fatigue.

fatigue

In its early stages, fatigue causes irritation – a period when the driver becomes niggled by delays and the activities of other road users. Becoming impatient and irritated by the traffic will make you fell stressed (and upset your passengers) and will not get you to your destination more quickly – it is also likely to cause you to make mistakes.

Fatigue in driving is partly due to prolonged muscular contraction, caused by sitting in an incorrect posture, or by tension from anxiety. While muscles are contracted, their blood vessels are compressed and this reduces their supply of oxygen and nutrients and slows down the removal of waste products from the muscle cells. Muscle fatigue gets worse and worse if the person remains in the same position.

passengers

Stress can be caused by the passengers, particularly children. Passengers should not nag, and should aim to make the driver's task as easy as possible; children should be taught never to distract the driver. They are less likely to do this if they sit in the back and are given games and activities. If they do create a disturbance, or get noisy, the driver should stop the car as soon as possible, explaining that it is not safe to drive in those conditions.

personality factors

The act of driving itself can have a profound effect on people. Not only do aggressive people become more so, but people who are normally civilised and restrained may suddenly reveal a savage side. Being inside the car, shut off from other people, acts as a form of insulation and this makes aggression safer because there is no face to face confrontation. Also, it is easy to impute hostile and negative feelings to the other driver: people can work up quite a hate feeling for the driver in the car behind or in front of them, take it as a personal insult if someone overtakes them (especially in a less powerful car, or a woman driver) and then try to make it hard for the driver concerned. Such retaliation not only causes extra stress but is dangerous.

Driving can be stressful even for people who are not subject to stress in other areas of their lives. For a few, however, going for a drive can help them to unwind when they are tense or angry.

what to do

Drive your own car carefully, calmly, competently and courteously, and hope that others will do likewise.

Make sure you are comfortable behind the wheel; check that your shoulders are not contracted and hunched, that your neck is not jutting forward, your teeth not clenched and your hands (both of them) holding, but not tightly gripping, the wheel.

Relax the shoulder muscles, take care that your back is well supported, relax your jaw and face muscles. When held up at a traffic light, relieve neck tension by small circling movements of your head, or try to practise slow breathing and tell yourself to relax as you breathe out.

It is helpful if you can find time to relax before you being a long drive, even a few minutes are better than nothing. Obviously, it is better to set out fresh, having had adequate sleep the night before, and to be neither hungry nor too replete.

You should try not to drive for more than 3 hours without a break. An overtired driver gets more and more uncomfortable and starts to lose concentration. It is important to allow for regular brief stops, some of which could include eating something (a biscuit will do, or an apple would be better) and a precautionary pee. If you stop at a layby or service area, go for a short walk to exercise the muscles and stimulate blood circulation, or even have a short nap. A tired driver is a danger to himself and to other road users.

A driver who becomes fatigued when it is unsafe to stop should open the car window and ventilators, turn on the radio and talk to passengers – or even himself. Obviously, he should break the journey as soon as possible.

Be particularly careful when driving home at the end of a long and tiring day, slow down a little if you normally tend to be a fast driver.

ROSPA, the Royal Society for the Prevention of Accidents, warns against car phones. Not only is there the distraction of dialling and answering while driving (both unlawful if the handset is held), but also because of the unknown news you may receive – for example, your wife phoning to say that Johnny has fallen into the canal.

accidents

Some accident-prone people appear always to be having accidents of one kind or another – on the road, in the home, at work. Some accidents are genuinely fortuitous, others are due to stupidity or bravado or lack of foresight, or stress.

Stress can predispose towards accidents in several ways: by making the person more preoccupied and forgetful, failing to carry out routine safety procedures. Someone worrying about problems at home or at work is not giving his full attention to what he is doing or to his immediate surroundings. Stress and anxiety may be associated with lack of co-ordination of movements, shakiness and clumsiness.

holidays and travel

Holidays are rated as a stress-related event, largely because there is a loss of everyday control – particularly if abroad over food, money, language – and general unfamiliarity. There is the danger of tempers erupting, particularly where there are children and heat. Amongst the reasons for family holiday stress is too much togetherness, too much luggage, and worry about the home that has been left behind.

For some people, holiday stress can be reduced by going to the same place every year, so then it is familiar, a home from home. Other people need to avoid building up expectations by having an impulsive surprise holiday, so that there is nothing to live up to, and therefore no disappointment.

It is better not to be too ambitious in what you attempt on holiday. Do not turn what should be a relaxing, regenerative experience into a major expedition that produces its own stresses. A self-catering or camping holiday may be no relaxation for the chief cook and bottle washer; nor may too much driving for the chauffeur.

Travelling by road has the stresses of traffic jams, long hot hours in restricted space; when taking a car abroad, the anxiety about arriving at the docks on time and driving on the 'wrong' side of the road. Traffic queues to embark, and often general exhaustion, contribute to the stress.

With all forms of travelling by public transport, there is the stress of the close proximity of strangers.

flying

When travelling by air, there is the noise and bustle of the airport terminal, flight delays or cancellations, the drawn-out procedures of check-in, security checks, baggage retrieval and so on.

Flying itself creates a certain amount of stress. The artificial environment of the aircraft flight cabin can affect body metabolisms: dehydration is a specific problem and can be counteracted by drinking plenty of liquid before setting out, and during the flight. On long flights, however, it is important to avoid alcohol, coffee and carbonated drinks because the discomfort of dehydration is exaggerated by these.

For some people, flying causes great anxiety because of claustrophobia, terror of heights, and being out of control. Relaxation techniques are effective in combating these fears. In London, air travel anxiety seminars are held at Guys Hospital.

jet-lag

Jet-lag is a specific condition set up by flying between time zones which force the body's biological clock out of step with the natural circadian rhythms of daylight and darkness. On arriving at the destination, it is better not to be tempted into an immediate therapeutic nap; keep going until the local bed-time, or take as little sleep as possible until the night after landing. This comparatively rough treatment should help shake the internal clock into following the local time.

There is a useful formula for the number of days needed to recover from jet-lag: divide the number of hours' difference between your starting point and your destination by two to give the basic number of recovery days needed, then add a day if you are travelling from west to east, or subtract a day if you are travelling from east to west. Research for NATO has found that with increasing age, increased recovery time is needed.

it's not all stress

In spite of the stress factors of actually taking a holiday, holidays are important. A holiday lends perspective to problems, they can then be seen for what they are. Even if you do not go away, having a holiday at home, perhaps with day excursions, is a stress-reducing manoeuvre.

Some lucky people have regular holidays once or even twice a year, and punctuate the rest of the time by long weekends. Some townspeople travel into the country every weekend, cycling or walking or visiting historic homes and gardens, when a longer holiday is impossible. Travel and holidays are still good bargains in terms of stress reduction.

crime

Financial pressure may lead to a person taking an ill-paid job without prospects, or drifting into petty crime. Crime and vandalism are a major source of stress. Burglary is also increasing; being burgled is an especial stress. At least the common-sense precautions of good locks (and using them!) may deter the casual opportunist burglar (maybe a teenager on the loose), and avoid unnecessary stress.

Where elderly people are afraid to leave their home unaccompanied because of the risk of being robbed or mugged, a neighbour's offer of help is a personal good deed and can help towards better community spirit.

Ø **The National Association of Victims Support Schemes**, Cranmer House, 39 Brixton Road, London SW9 5DZ (telephone 01-326 1084) has over three hundred local victims support schemes which offer emotional or practical support where needed, to people who have suffered through crime. Often the effects of a crime are long-lasting.

Anyone seeking help can find the address of the local scheme from the police or citizens advice bureau, or from the headquarters of the Association.

prison sentence

The life event with the fourth-highest stress rating in the stress chart is what in the USA is called 'jail term'.

Most offenders do not assume they will be caught. The stress begins with being detected, before any sentence, let alone imprisonment. Stress is exacerbated when family and friends find out about the whole matter in court. Even then, the prospect of prison is not expected: a person goes to court expecting to be cautioned, fined or given probation, not sent to gaol.

When an accused goes to court, he should go prepared to be sentenced. (Remember, you might be remanded.) Anticipatory anxiety – similar to warming up before a run – is one of the best ways to cope with the prospect of imprisonment.

The Prison Rules (SI No. 1964/388 and amendments) can be bought from HMSO, the Stationery Office. They give you an idea of your rights, whether convicted or unconvicted (that is, remanded in custody), rights about what to wear in prison (your own clothes if on remand), about food (can be sent in if on remand), and so on. But do not take the rules with you to court, nor talk about having read them.

The actual experience of prison may not be as bad as expected, particularly if you expect the worst. In some respects, prison might be a relief for the kind of people who feel they need to be punished, which is a not insignificant number.

If you have been in a total institution, such as boarding school, crew of a ship, or uniformed services, or in long-term hospital care, that is a precedent to work on. In some respects, prison is relaxing: decisions, for example, about what to wear, what time to get up, what to eat are made for you.

Officers (not to be called warders), will expect you to call them 'sir' (or 'madam'). There is no need to be servile, but do collaborate. You are wasting your breath by arguing.

Some stressors inherent in the system are being with others not of your choosing, three people in a cell. Letters are restricted. All letters, ingoing and outgoing are read by prison officials. This is fundamentally a security measure. In time you will come to terms with this. Visits are restricted. No-one is allowed to visit until the prisoner has sent out a 'visiting order', on which the visitor has been named (there is space for three names on the order).

the family

There is another person serving the prisoner's sentence: the one(s) left behind who also need to be prepared.

Serving the second sentence: a survival guide for wife and families of prisoners by Dave J. Hardwick (£4.50 PEPAR publications, 50 Knightlow Road, Harborne, Birmingham B17 8QB) is written by a prisoner. It gives much useful straightforward advice; details of sources of support; how to keep in touch – with the warning to be careful not to visit a prisoner without a visiting order from the prisoner. Similarly, be careful about the number of letters you write and to some extent the length, as this may intrude on the ration of letters permitted.

Where the sentence is a long one, the local probation service will, in all probability, provide what is called 'through care' – that is, they will keep in touch with the person serving the sentence with a view to offering voluntary (or providing compulsory) aftercare on discharge. This through-care should also provide some help to relatives, if only in order to establish some sort of home or accommodation when the sentence has ended.

Remission is automatic on all sentences, but to begin with forget that, and think in terms of the months or years that the court has ordered. Expect the worst, in that way reality will be less stressful.

STRESS AT WORK

Increasing stress, from whatever source, may show itself as inability to cope at work. The person's performance suffers and he may flit from one task to another unable to concentrate sufficiently on any one. Increasing stress may produce a rise in general activity which may become uncoordinated or arbitrary, with much energy expended on unproductive tasks; this in turn increases the stress. The person becomes irritable and impulsive and may do unexpected and ill-considered things.

We spend a major part of our waking life at work. Often people are identified by the work they do: he is an architect; she is a professor of anthropology; he is a plumber. Some people introduce themselves by saying what they do for a living. Work is a most valuable source of satisfaction as well as stress. Thus what happens to us at work is important to our health and sense of well being. Losing a job is not only losing a source of income.

EXAMPLES OF WORK STRESSORS

too much work
change in work practice
competing deadlines
responsibility without authority
unclear goals
boss with abrasive communication
 style
lack of leadership in times of crisis
inadequate rewards – low salary,
 poor prospects
promotion or demotion
threat of redundancy
hostile customers
incompetent co-workers
irritating supervisor
transfer involving move to different
 area
new management style
technological change
too many meetings

sexual harassment at work
boring monotonous work
shift work
piecework remuneration leading to
 unhealthy competition
uncomfortable uniforms
too much noise
interruptions by telephone calls
inadequate lighting, heating or
 ventilation
equipment breakdowns
insubordinate juniors
little opportunity for learning new
 things
office politics
unclear line of authority
mistrust of those in power
imposed changes from above
 without consultation.

It is important to recognise potential sources of stress at work, under what circumstances these are likely to affect one's health and optimum functioning, so as to cope better.

Work-related stress is considered less harmful than other stresses such as death or divorce. But because people spend such a long time at work, the difficulties they encounter can be intensified so as to reach unmanageable proportions. The realisation that stress-related illness not only means hardship to individuals but costs the country millions in terms of days lost has led to a growing interest in the causes of stress and a search for ways to alleviate it.

Researches in the 1970's regarded dull, boring, repetitive work as the major cause of stress at work. It was felt that factory workers trying to keep up with an assembly line were particularly at risk, especially as shift work compounded the difficulties by affecting the body's natural rhythms.

In the last ten years, however, there has been more research into stress at work, and it is now believed that a variety of factors are responsible, and that personality plays a major role in whether stress becomes distress.

A number of studies on different areas of work to determine their stress potential have identified several key factors:

○ factors intrinsic to the job
○ role in the organisation
○ career prospects
○ relations within the organisation
○ the home/work interface.

factors intrinsic to the job

Not surprisingly, a number of 'high risk' professions have been identified, such as air traffic controller, airline pilot, medical staff, also city executives. Stress may show simply as irritability, but may lead to irrational or wrong decisions with far-reaching consequences. Factors which can also cause considerable stress are long hours, adverse working conditions and 'overwork'. The increasing incidence of stress amongst teachers may in part be attributable to long-running pay disputes threatening to undermine their personal sense of worth and dignity. Pupil indiscipline is less of a stress factor than trying to motivate disinterested pupils, and poor working conditions, poor commercial prospects, increased pressure from parents all lead to what is now called 'teacher burn-out'.

According to World Health Organisation figures, blue-collar workers run a higher risk of coronaries and heart disease directly linked to high levels of stress than executives do. There is evidence that, in potentially dangerous work environments, stress can cause accidents and serious injuries among blue-collar workers. Companies, when recruiting, tend to reserve psychological testing for managers, and test blue-collar workers for basic technical skills.

technology
The introduction of new technology can affect staff at all levels. Even when the technique has been mastered, the operator may face more, or at least different, physical demands on eyes and back muscles and may face the fear of the equipment breaking down and eventually higher levels of boredom.

A meticulous person may find it stressful to work on an assembly line at a set pace which does not give him the opportunity to check the quality of the work. By contrast, a brilliant improviser may be irked by having to do things by the book.

shift work
Shift work incorporates stresses of a particular kind. The body has very definite, built-in, daily rhythms. For example, the secretion of the hormone cortisol (hydrocortisone) which protects against stress effects, is lowest during sleep. With shift work (as in jet-lag), these rhythms are disrupted and the shift-worker has bodily stresses added to any psychological ones. People who are on permanent or long term night shifts are much less stressed than those who work a cycle of 2 or 3 different shifts every few weeks. However, the unsociable hours associated with permanent early, late or night shifts can also constitute a stress.

interaction

Some jobs involve contact and even conflict with people who are themselves stressed. For example, traffic wardens encounter harassed motorists looking for somewhere to park, bus conductors have to face long queues of angry commuters who in their own stress do not realise that it is not fair to take it out on people who are only doing their job; a doctor is expected to reassure an anxious sick person, a social worker to deal with a family under stress. A recent study of the police force found out that the physically gruesome part of the job, such as road traffic accidents or dealing with violent people were less stressful than the tremendous amount of paper work for which they had not been trained, and court appearances.

role in the organisation and career prospects

Lack of clarity in one's job, either in role or function, can be particularly stressful. Support staff may feel less 'important' than front line staff; similarly, voluntary or part-time workers may feel inferior to paid or full-time employees. Uncertainty is also felt to be a primary cause of stress.

Staff who feel unable to contribute to the decision-making process may feel frustrated; lack of effective communication, lack of autonomy and 'office politics' may create considerable pressure. Often it is the second-in-command rather than the boss who is stressed: he may find it difficult, if not impossible, to question his instructions or to control his workload. Companies that encourage participation are likely to have better employee and organisational health than those that do not. It is now known that stress can be combated by giving employees more of a say in the work place.

Upward progression is still regarded as the norm and many staff feel cheated when promotion ceases or takes longer than anticipated. In the current climate, where many organisations are contracting rather than expanding, promotion prospects may be considerably reduced. Allied to this are the difficulties connected with mobility, early retirement or redeployment, or even redundancy.

relations within the organisation

Interpersonal relations at all levels within the organisation can contribute to stress. Staff in dispute with their boss may feel under permanent pressure, while conflict with one's subordinates, for whatever reason, can be very destructive of the individual.

Contact with colleagues can provoke very negative emotions which have to be suppressed because of having to work side-by-side. Most people have very little say in the choice of their workmates. A pool of secretaries may be disrupted and stressed by a fussy or a slovenly or lazy newcomer. In dangerous jobs, lack of full trust in a workmate is particularly stressful because a lapse on his part may endanger others.

Where a person is aware that others who are technically 'under' him think that they could do the job as well, if not better, the consequent self-doubt is a source of stress – for the foreman on the shop floor as much as for the conductor of an orchestra.

women

Women face extra stresses when they are in occupations traditionally thought of as 'man's work' or in management position.

Career progression is a source of considerable frustration to women who may feel hampered by their domestic circumstances or by having taken a career break. As the number of women in executive employment increases, so does the incidence of stress-related illness such as heart disease and ulcers amongst women, and also cancer.

Women in many parts of the country are under financial pressure to return to work or to combine motherhood with employment. Few families conform to the advertisers' stereotype of dad at work and mum at home and at least one family in eight has only one parent, usually a woman.

The pressures women face include the difficulties of balancing home and work, perceived or real discrimination, guilt and often low pay and status, resulting in a lack of confidence and feeling of no value.

Even a carefully worked out division of a woman's time between family and work leaves her without essential restorative periods of time to herself.

The woman with a family can suffer recurring anxiety about her children returning to an empty house and guilt because she is too busy catching up with domestic chores, or simply too tired to listen to her family's problems.

Women are intrinsically conscientious and a sense of not giving herself wholly to her work may pervade a woman's consciousness even when she is giving at least as much as her male colleagues.

employer/employee

The employer has important powers over his employees even though these powers are governed or curtailed by legislation about security of employment and by union rules. The employer can sometimes make conditions of work so stressful for an employee he wishes to get rid of that the employee leaves of his or her own accord. The employee is in an ambivalent relationship with his employer: on the one hand he is indebted to his employer for his livelihood (particularly during periods of high unemployment), on the other, he may have grievances about his salary, promotion prospects, status, perks, lack of consideration.

Where the real employer is a statutory body, faceless and unapproachable to the average employee, and the apparent employer is merely an agent, for example for the local authority or the health service, he has responsibility for the employee without real power. If problems arise, both find the situation stressful. There are arbitration and appeal procedures which may help to defuse such situations but they are elaborate or, in some cases, inadequate.

Even a sympathetic employer or personnel officer may not appreciate how stressful a job or part of a job can be. Identifying which component of the job contributes most to the stress, and making even quite small modifications, may reduce the stress.

Making counselling available to workers can lead to a dramatic drop in stress-related problems.

Ø **The Mental Health Foundation**, 8 Hallam Street, London W1N 6DH (telephone 01-580 0145) has published a booklet *Someone to talk to at work* which includes the message: the question you should be asking those members of staff who are clearly not happy, and therefore not doing their work as well as they should, is "What is the problem?", or "Would you like to talk about it?" If they want someone to talk to, you may well be that someone, at least to start with.

The Training Division of the Cabinet Office has published a 4-part series (£9.95 each, from HMSO) *Understanding Stress* as a resource and working tool to assist all those who have an interest in stress, either from their own point of view or from the point of view of someone who works with or manages other people.

the workaholic

Overwork not only causes stress but may itself be a symptom of stress, arising from work or reflecting problems at home or in the family. For instance, strained personal relationships can lead to an escape into (over)work.

Overwork manifests itself as long hours, not always productive, hurried meal breaks, or missed meals, taking work home (if the work is of that type), and reluctance to take short breaks or longer holidays, which sets up a vicious circle of stress. Other symptoms include: difficulty or unwillingness to delegate, work problems affecting sleep, giving up pastimes because of work commitments.

A person may find himself unable to cope with his work, either because of intrinsic inadequacies, or because new technologies are making increasing demands on him, or because he has been promoted too rapidly and too far. The 'Peter principle' states that in a hierarchy every employee tends to rise to his level of incompetence, that is, being promoted away from a job he can accomplish, to one just outside his competence. At that level, whether the incompetence is appreciated by the person or not, stress results because the job is now in essence impossible. Overwork and frustration lead to a build-up of major stress which may be the trigger which precipitates a heart attack.

the stages

It is sometimes possible to trace three stages in 'executive burn-out' (the workaholic's stress syndrome). To begin with, all is excitement and the flow of adrenalin is put to good use, the jobs get done and more is taken on. Then things start getting out of control: anxiety and a feeling of being driven set in, the hours worked get longer to keep up the momentum. Some of the warning signals are migraine, stomach trouble, twitches, and relief may be sought in drugs or drink. The final phase reflects the person's disintegration – more time is needed to perform the set tasks, a vicious circle sets in.

For some people, even when the goals have been reached, it may be difficult to ease up. Years of striving for promotion and recognition have become a way of life, and a deliberate effort has to be made to lessen the pressures.

A conscious effort has to be made to learn to relax (the world will go on even without your working $16\frac{1}{2}$ hours a day), proper breathing, good posture, perhaps autogenic exercises, massage all help.

what can be done about stress at work

There are a number of things individuals can do to alleviate stress at work – both for themselves and for others:

○ encourage an understanding of what stress is and what can cause it; recognising it as an acceptable part of work can make it less of a taboo subject

○ try to improve communication in the workplace and encourage participation at all levels

○ help all staff to maximise their potential through relevant training and development programmes

○ encourage attendance at workshops or courses that assist staff to reduce pressure on themselves, such as time management and effective work practices

○ help everyone to develop self-confidence – provide or ask for regular feedback sessions on performance.

Ø **The Stress Foundation**, 1 Speldhurst Court, Queen's Road, Maidstone, Kent ME16 0JN (telephone 0622 681498) was formed for the express purpose of developing a scientific multidisciplinary approach to the understanding and control of stress in industrial societies, and of presenting it to industry and the public at large in terms understandable by the layman. It offers study days and courses on stress management; courses can be tailored to meet the needs of a particular organisation or industry. They can include video and audio programmes, together with relaxation tapes. Personnel can be trained to give courses throughout their own organisation. The fees vary according to the client's requirements.

attitudes

Work is not only important for obvious economic reasons but, for many people, bound up with a deeply ingrained work ethic and a way of proving themselves. If they cannot do so, particularly if they feel that promotion is being unjustifiably withheld, the stress of feeling overlooked is then followed by

the stress of wondering whether the failure to achieve promotion might indeed reflect personal inadequacies.

A change in attitude may be needed rather than any change
in the nature of the work itself, or its environment. If you
realise that, for you, the job is no more than a 9 to 5 routine
which pays the bills, this may lessen stressful aspects. If your
work is the centre point of your life and the job has become
unsatisfying or seems full of stress, a salutary exercise might be
to imagine how you would feel if tomorrow you were told that
you have to stop being in the job (perhaps being made redun-
ant). Such a thought might help to put some of the difficulties
into perspective.

unemployment

There is a strong link between unemployment and ill health
and between unemployment and earlier death, including
death from heart disease. There is also a correlation between
unemployment and higher rates of admission to mental hospitals and prisons, more deaths, suicides and murders.

The stress is due not only to loss of income but to the loss of
shared experiences and contact with people outside the home,
and to the loss of identity associated with one's job. This can
quickly turn to a feeling of futility, and a lack of confidence
about one's ability to get a job or to hold one down if offered.
If, after a while, the unemployed person loses heart, he may
become poorly motivated to seek work. Marital friction may
develop or increase through being cooped up all day or if the
wife becomes the only breadwinner.

the stages

There are stages in people's psychological reaction to becoming unemployed after being in work. At first there is shock and
disbelief, but tempered with a certain optimism and sense of
being on holiday. Then follows a sense of meaningless leisure,

inertia and exhaustion, with a loss of self-esteem, anxiety and depression, and tensions in the family. Generally, prolonged unemployment means a significant decline in standard of living – which leads to stress related to the obvious economic problems. Lastly comes a chronic state of passive acceptance marked by submissiveness, a feeling of inferiority, a lack of identity, a restricted way of life and little hope of change.

Long-term (over a year) unemployment is less acutely stressful than short-term loss of job, but can lead to depression and even to physical ill health. Young people who are out of work generally accept their lot but it puts great strains on family relationships. Research into youth unemployment showed that young women display greater feelings of anger about their situation and that mothers carry the brunt of the family pressures in the home. Young men did not have the same sense of isolation and anger felt by young women.

counselling

Unemployment counselling is sometimes available, though this is probably more likely in areas of high unemployment. RELATE (previously the National Marriage Guidance Council) centres offer help to couples whose problems are due to the strain of unemployment.

Finance and debt counselling services are available in many areas, provided by the citizens advice bureaux and other agencies. It is best to go to the CAB first; if there is a more appropriate centre locally, the CAB will tell you.

Ø **Housing Debtline** Birmingham (telephone 021 359 8501) is a national telephone advice service on housing debts and is a joint project of the Birmingham Settlement and the Money Advice Association. It gives expert advice over the telephone and can back this up with a self-help information pack sent to the caller free of charge. This pack will tell you how to
○ work out your personal budget
○ deal with priority debts
○ work out offers of payment to creditors
○ deal with court papers and procedures.

using your time

Unemployment leaves people without a structured day or daily pattern. This increases stress. It is wise to get up at a reasonable fixed time, perhaps the same time as when going to work; meals should be at regular times.

It is also important to keep as fit as possible while unemployed. This should be easy as there is more time for exercise or sport. But, paradoxically, a great deal of discipline is necessary (it helps to set aside a regular time). Exercise has the extra advantage of being a good antidote for stress.

It may be possible to find some part-time or occasional work which would continue the link to the working population and help to avoid the social isolation of the out-of-work.

If no money-earning activities seem available, it could be a good idea to use the time to develop a useful skill (such as typing, bricklaying, a foreign language, cooking) which might be put to profitable use later, even after retirement.

retirement

Retirement marks a new phase in life. It is a time for taking stock and making certain decisions about the future. Some people see retirement as a happy release, for others the end of their working life seems the end of their useful life. Added to this are usually financial worries, the pension may be a great deal less than previous earnings. People may have no friends outside work and suffer the stress of loneliness and may simply have no idea what to do with themselves all day. Boredom and lack of stimulation certainly cause stress.

Not only can the stresses of retirement be made worse by lack of resources and reserves, eventually the pensioner may lose a spouse and be unable to face socialising as a single person.

Ø **The Pre-Retirement Association of Great Britain and Northern Ireland**, 19 Undine Street, London SW17 8PP (telephone 01-767 3225) gives support and help for those who are going to retire or are retired.

voluntary work

People often complain that they do not have the time to do things they would like. The enforced leisure of unemployment or retirement could well be used to do some of these things though, surprisingly, it will require considerable self-discipline.

Finding some form of voluntary work gives a sense of usefulness and the satisfaction of being with others: helping with children or old people, giving help in a hospital, especially if there is a league of friends; helping to teach someone to read. Make sure, if you are going to do voluntary work, that it is something you will enjoy and that you will not end up being out of pocket (ask for your expenses to be covered).

Local libraries and the local social services departments usually have details of organisations needing help and may co-ordinate volunteers in the locality.

People interested in voluntary work should contact their local volunteer bureau or council for voluntary service (or, in country areas, community council or council of community service). These will be listed in Yellow Pages under social service and welfare organisations. Details of volunteer bureaux or of councils for voluntary service or of community councils can be obtained from

Ø **National Council for Voluntary Organisations**, 26 Bedford Square, London WC1B 3HU (telephone 01-636 4066) or from

Ø **The Volunteer Centre**, 29 Lower Kings Road, Berkhamsted, Herts HP4 2AB (telephone 04427-73311).

Ø **Age Endeavour Fellowship**, Willowthorpe, High Street, Stanstead Abbots, nr. Ware, Hertfordshire SG12 8AS (telphone 0920 870158) is a charity concerned with employment and activity in retirement. Also sets up Buretire employment bureaux for the newly-retired who are seeking employment in local industry.

STRESS-RELATED DISEASES

Research (in the United States and Australia) has found some small correlation between stress-inducing life events and subsequent frequency, severity and duration of several disorders, including colds, 'flu, tuberculosis and various allergies. Research is going on into evidence that stress impairs the immune system: it is thought by some that high levels of stress may depress the body's immune system, making illness more likely.

In any case, some illnesses are believed to be related to stress, at least in part, in some people. In some, stress seems to be the most important factor. In others, stress is not the major factor but can make the condition worse or make bouts or attacks more likely to occur.

allergy

An allergy is a reaction to a substance which in itself is normally not harmful, called an allergen. The most common are pollens from flowers and trees, household pets, certain foodstuffs such as shellfish and strawberries – but an allergen can be almost anything. The reaction includes hay fever, itching, a rash, nasal streaming, joint pains, wheezing. Many of the symptoms of allergy are due to the release of histamine into the blood stream.

Some, but not all, sufferers find that their attacks are more frequent or more severe under conditions of stress. Sometimes symptoms are attributed to psychological stress when they are really allergic reactions – and the reverse can be the case.

Once something has triggered off an allergy, the person is likely to go on being sensitive to whatever substance has caused it. Treatment is generally by antihistamine drugs.

angina pectoris

The heart needs a continuous flow of blood to supply it with oxygen and nutrients so that it can work. The blood flows to the heart through the coronary arteries. If they become narrowed by the deposition of fatty substances in the wall of the blood vessel (atheroma), the blood supply is impeded and the supply of oxygen jeopardised. If there is an inadequate blood supply through the coronary arteries and an extra load is put on it (for instance during exercise, in cold weather, or following a large meal), the person may suffer an anginal attack. Angina is a gripping pain across the chest and sometimes into the neck and jaw or down the arm. When there is no longer an extra demand, such as on stopping exercise, the pain goes away after a few minutes.

Anxiety, fear and stress may bring on anginal attacks. In an emotional crisis, there is an increased release of the hormones adrenaline and noradrenaline into the blood stream, which increases the force and speed of the heart, and so increases the work of the heart. Spasms of the blood vessels may well be stress induced. This is a significant factor in bringing on angina in people with coronary artery disease; the same effect can also occur even in people whose arteries are completely clear.

The pain of the angina can then constitute a stress in its own right. The person becomes afraid of having anginal attacks; this heightened anxiety makes attacks more likely.

Drugs can be taken when an attack occurs. The drug usually used to dilate the blood vessels is glyceryl trinitrate (trinitrin) which is dissolved in the mouth at the onset of an attack; other anti-anginal drugs such as the beta-blockers reduce the oxygen demand and the number of heartbeats per minute. Or, instead of a beta-blocking drug, the doctor may prescribe calcium blockers to prevent attacks of angina.

asthma

In an attack of asthma, the tubes through which air is carried in and out of the lungs (the mucosa) become narrowed. This is caused by contraction of the muscles in the wall of the tube and by the secretion of a sticky mucus in the tubes themselves. As a result, it becomes more and more difficult to get air into and out of the lungs. The symptoms are shortness of breath, wheezing and cough. The worse the breathlessness, the greater is the feeling of anxiety, which in turn may worsen or prolong the attack.

Attacks can be precipitated by allergies, chest infections, irritant fumes, and psychological factors. Stress does not 'cause' asthma, but in some people it is the initiating factor; in others, stress is the factor which prolongs the attack. Often it is a combination of factors that produces an attack. Possibly, stress brings about a change in the bronchial mucosa and in the pattern of breathing; genetic factors may contribute.

If stress can contribute to attacks of asthma, reducing stress should be of benefit. There is evidence that training in relaxation, not repressing anger and not panicking when minor changes in breathing occur, reduces an asthma sufferer's attacks.

There is an old belief that over-anxious mothers contribute to their children's asthma, but this has not been scientifically substantiated. Where there are psychological factors, such as the parent's over-protectiveness or the child's using attacks to get attention, family counselling may help to lessen the degree of stress.

Ø **Asthma Society and Friends of the Asthma Research Council**, 300 Upper Street, London N1 2XX (telephone 01-226 2260) publishes a variety of booklets and pamphlets and has local branches which hold meetings and offer help and information to individual sufferers and their families.

baldness

Acute patchy hairlessness (alopecia areata) is a form of acute baldness in which hair falls out in handfuls. The scalp hair falls out, and also eyebrows and body hair. The alopecia may be localised, so that the person develops bald patches. The cause of alopecia is uncertain. Some sufferers can relate it to episodes of stress, especially in initial attacks, but in other people the connection is less clear. The hair will usually grow again.

cancer

Much remains to be discovered about the cause or causes of cancer. It is probable that cancer has not a single cause but where a number of risk factors apply to a person, there is greater likelihood that cancer will develop. A theory which is being followed up by researchers is that emotional factors, such as stress, could be a contributing factor in some cancers (for example, that stress altering hormone levels may, perhaps, promote breast cancer). So far, well-controlled studies have failed to support the hypothesis that cancer is one of the diseases in which the functioning of the body may become affected by physical changes associated with disturbed mental or emotional processes.

If emotional factors were to contribute to the development or course of some kinds of cancer, such an effect would be brought about by biological mechanisms. It has been suggested that the body's immune responses, which defend it against cancer cells, may be impaired by stress. Stress induces secretion of adrenaline and noradrenaline and it is possible that these hormones, in turn, tend to suppress or reduce certain immune responses. However, it is highly likely that many complex mechanisms are involved; the biological pathways linking emotional factors with cancer remain to be discovered.

The Consumers' Association's book *Understanding cancer*

gives a balanced and factual account of the nature, causes and treatment (conventional and complementary) of cancer and includes details of self-help and support groups and other relevant organisations.

diabetes mellitus

Acute symptoms of diabetes may occur for the first time following physical illness or injury or an emotional crisis. Diabetes may first be noticed at the time of a heart attack and persist after the patient has recovered from his heart disease. Although it seems doubtful whether diabetes can actually be caused by physical or emotional stress, it may be that a stress can bring into the open diabetes that was hitherto hidden, rather than provoking diabetes in a previously normal individual.

In someone already under treatment for diabetes, both physical and emotional stress can cause a worsening, but individuals vary greatly in their susceptibility. Physical stresses such as infections, heart attacks, accidents, can provoke the symptoms of untreated diabetes, in particular thirst and excessive urine flow. Less is known about the effects of emotional stress. Where it leads to worsening of the condition, this may be due as much to the person's reduced attention to the details of the treatment regime as to a direct effect on the body metabolism.

Adolescents with diabetes, in particular, may react against the restrictions of the treatment regime or may, consciously or unconsciously, use their diabetes as a weapon in their relationships with other family members or with people outside the family.

Like any chronic disorder, diabetes can give rise to emotional stresses, particularly when the diagnosis is first made.

Ø **British Diabetic Association**, 10 Queen Anne Street, London W1M 0BD (telephone 01-323 1531) has over 300 groups which hold regular meetings and give support locally, provides practical help and information for people with diabetes and their families; publishes a wide range of leaflets, books and videos. *Balance*, the BDA magazine (free to members) includes medical news, recipe ideas, local events and articles on living with diabetes.

Ø **National Diabetes Foundation**, 177a Tennison Road, London SE25 5NF (telephone 01-656 5467) has local branches and a 24-hour answering service, particularly useful for the newly-diagnosed, also for parents of diabetic children during the evening and at weekends; can help with stressful family situations, pregnancy, diet, etc.; runs holidays for diabetic children and welfare services for the elderly.

heart attack

When the blood supply to the heart muscle is abruptly stopped, this causes a heart attack. It is generally due to clotting in a coronary blood vessel, that is, one surrounding the heart and supplying it with blood. Stress can contribute to this – clotting of the blood takes place by a complex mechanism and stress factors increase the stickiness of blood making it more likely to clot.

A stressful existence leads to the sustained production of the hormones adrenaline and noradrenaline which, among other things, mobilise fatty acids which are a source of energy. In the absence of exercise to burn up these fatty substances, it is thought that they accumulate and interact with other fatty substances to form atheroma, a deposit in the wall of blood vessels. (This is particularly critical in blood vessels close to the heart and in the brain and kidneys.)

Heart attacks are dramatic events and doctors can monitor the changes in the electrical activity of the heart; many studies have therefore been carried out. The results link heart attacks to a variety of psychological, physical and other factors. Cigarette smoking predisposes the individual to heart attacks (about doubling the risk); gross degrees of overweight are associated with an increased incidence of heart attack. Lack of exercise is another factor, and so is too much drastic exercise. Probably it is the interaction of factors which is important: smoking, heredity, high blood pressure, diet with a high intake of saturated fats, as in meat and dairy products – and stress.

type A, type B
Attempts have been made to relate the likelihood of a heart attack to personality types. Two American researchers, Friedman and Rosenman, divided their subjects (all men) into two groups: type A people with a chronic sense of time-urgency, are aggressive, ambitious, driving themselves on to meet (often self-imposed) deadlines. They are self-demanding, often doing two or three things at once, impatient and always in a hurry.

They are likely to react with hostility to anything that seems to get in their way and are temperamentally incapable of letting go. They are also likely to think they are indispensable. All this adds up to a state of constant stress.

Type B men exhibit opposite characteristics, being less competitive, less preoccupied with achievement, less rushed and generally more easygoing, not allowing their lives to be governed by a series of deadlines. They are also better at separating work from play, and know how to relax. They are less prone to anger, and do not feel constantly impatient, rushed and under pressure.

The type A and type B story is now almost folklore and is still taught to medical students because it is such a nice piece of research. However, A and B are not strict prototypes but indicate patterns of behaviour shown by certain people in our society. Most people are not straight As or Bs but a mixture, with type A or B predominating.

It used to be thought that the incidence of heart attacks was much higher in type A than in type B individuals. But, for reasons that are obscure, the Friedman and Rosenman findings do not seem to apply with much force in the UK: attempts to repeat the work in Europe have not proved anything.

Ø **The Coronary Prevention Group**, 60 Great Ormond Street, London WC1N 3HR (telephone 01-833 3687) whose work is dedicated to the prevention of coronary heart disease, provides information and practical advice about the major causes of the disease. Their publications include a range of booklets, briefing papers, policy documents and free fact sheets. Associate members (£10 per year) receive details of publications, seminars, conferences and a free quarterly newsletter.

high blood pressure (hypertension)

For many years it has been known, particularly to life insurance companies, that the higher the blood pressure, the more likely one is to die prematurely (compared to people with low blood pressure). High blood pressure can directly cause strokes, burst blood vessels resulting in brain haemorrhage; and when the pressure is high, the heart has to pump harder which can put it under strain. Moreover, blood pressure, along with cigarette smoking and abnormalities of blood lipids (fatlike substances) is associated with premature narrowing and hardening of the arteries which itself can produce heart attacks and strokes.

For the majority of people it is not understood what causes increase in blood pressure. Many factors are involved, particularly family history, probably a genetic or inherited characteristic, salt intake and, perhaps, intake of other minerals.

In most people, the blood pressure goes up and down greatly during the day in relation to emotion and exercise. There is evidence that acute stress is associated with a rise in blood pressure. In most cases, the blood pressure will revert to normal if the stress is removed. However, if the rise in blood pressure has been severe and prolonged, changes can take place in the arteries of the body which result in the raised blood pressure being maintained even after the stress has been reduced or removed.

Blood pressure may rise and become abnormal without any symptoms being noticed and is not necessarily related to red faces or dizziness. If you suffer from headaches, or unexplained fatigue and dizziness or palpitations, it is worth consulting your doctor. The only way of knowing what one's blood pressure is, is to have it measured. The results of treatment are good and many of the risks can be almost eliminated if the blood pressure can be returned to normal with treatment.

The Drug and Therapeutics Bulletin in an article on 'The treatment of mild hypertension' published in January 1988 said that

> "Treatment of high blood pressure should not always be undertaken with drugs. People with mild blood pressure should first give up smoking, lose weight and cut down on salt and alcohol. Trials of non-drug treatment have shown that almost one in two patients with mild blood pressure can control their problem for up to four years by losing five to ten pounds in weight, restricting salt intake, and restricting themselves to no more than two alcoholic drinks a day. Those who have to resort to drug treatment may manage with a lower dose of drug if they use other measures to control the problem. People with high blood pressure generally benefit from relaxation and stress reduction, whether or not they are taking drugs as well."

Raised blood pressure is by no means necessarily due to stress. But it makes sense for a person suffering from high blood pressure to examine his life style and attempt to change it if it is stressful.

irritable bowel syndrome

This condition, also called spastic colon or irritable colon syndrome, is very common and is now widely recognised. The symptoms are colicky pain, usually in the lower abdomen, variable bowel habit with periods of diarrhoea, constipation or both; distension of the abdomen, and occasionally belching or heartburn. Symptoms can come and go over long periods of time, and are often made worse by stress.

One theory is that irritable bowel syndrome may be caused primarily by a lack of residue in the diet. By the time the remnants of food, after absorption of nutrients, enter the colon (large bowel) they have insufficient bulk to be propelled easily downwards to the back passage. Instead of the small contractions required to squeeze a large bulk down the bowel, the colon has to squeeze very tightly to propel a small bulk. This may lead to spasm of the colon, which causes the pain; the lack of bulk produces either diarrhoea or small hard pellety stools. Stress can make the colon go into spasm, particularly if it contains insufficient bulk and this exacerbates irritable bowel syndrome.

The irritable bowel syndrome can be divided into two groups of sufferers: those where constipation dominates and those where there are other symptoms. Stress is probably less important than diet where the main symptom is constipation (which is particularly associated with lack of dietary fibre). For the remaining people, who have episodes of diarrhoea, and distension, stress features more prominently.

Drugs that relieve colonic spasm are sometimes prescribed at first, but generally irritable bowel syndrome is treated by trying to deal with the sources of stress, and by increasing the fibre content of the diet. This is best achieved by eating plenty of green vegetables and wholemeal bread.

In two less common diseases, ulcerative colitis and Crohn's disease, the bowel becomes ulcerated. The symptoms are attacks of diarrhoea containing mucus and blood; both diseases usually continue for years, with attacks often precipitated and exacerbated by stress. Treatment, usually under hospital supervision, involves the use of steroids and some other anti-inflammatory drugs. Obviating stress can help a great deal in avoiding frequent attacks.

migraine headaches

Although the term is sometimes used indiscriminately to refer to any severe, prostrating headache, migraine is a specific type of headache due to spasms and relaxations of blood vessels in the coverings of the brain.

The attack usually starts with a visual phenomenon (called an aura) which can take the form of flares around objects, or flashes of zig-zag patterns. The headache is severe, usually accompanied by nausea, vomiting, and great sensitivity to light. The pain may affect one side of the head only.

The mechanism of an attack of classical migraine is believed to be a constriction of the blood vessels supplying the brain followed by dilation. The first is supposed to produce the aura, the second the headache.

Some sufferers recognise that their attacks are closely related to episodes of tension and stress in their lives (even 'nice' stress can cause an attack). Relaxation techniques may help these sufferers and so may ordinary painkillers. Otherwise, treatment is mainly by drugs containing ergotamine which constricts the dilated blood vessels. It is helpful if the sufferer can sit or lie down in a quiet, dark room and, if possible, sleep.

Once a person has identified what triggers an attack, he may be able to avoid one. It is important to realise that two or three factors can act together and that one trigger does not always provoke an attack.

An article on headache was published in the magazine *Self-health*, March 1987.

Ø **The Migraine Trust**, 45 Great Ormond Street, London WC1N 3HD (telephone 01-278 2676) encourages and assists research into migraine. It publishes a booklet on migraine and a news sheet and can also give advice over the telephone.

Ø Sufferers from migraine can attend the **Princess Margaret Migraine Clinic**, Charing Cross Hospital, Fulham Palace Road, London W6 8RF (telephone 01-741 7833). They should first obtain a letter of referral from their doctor and then write for an appointment. Anyone who has a severe attack while in the vicinity of the clinic can, at any time, receive emergency treatment. They should ask for the casualty department and will be directed to a room where they will be seen by a doctor especially interested in migraine and where they can rest quietly.

Ø A similar service is offered by the **City of London Migraine Clinic**, 22 Charterhouse Square, London EC1 (telephone 01-251 3322).

In the provinces, a number of hospitals have an interest in migraine. Sufferers could ask their doctor to refer them to the department of neurology. The Migraine Trust is able to advise as to which hospitals have this particular interest.

Ø **British Migraine Association**, 178a High Road, Byfleet, Weybridge, Surrey KT14 7ED (telephone 09323 52468) is a registered charity run by migraine sufferers for migraine sufferers. Its aims are to encourage and support research into migraine and to distribute information about methods of controlling and relieving migraine. It publishes leaflets and a newsletter and offers a postal and telephone information service.

peptic ulcer

A peptic ulcer is a breach or defect in the lining of the upper part of the gut. Peptic ulcers are most common in the duodenum (the first part of the small intestine), but can also occur in the stomach (gastric ulcer) and the gullet (oesophageal ulcer). The commonest symptom of a peptic ulcer is pain. People with a peptic ulcer are often woken at night with their pain.

Many people with a gastric ulcer find that food makes their pain worse; those with a duodenal ulcer often find that their pain is brought on by hunger and relieved by eating. Pain from any type of ulcer is nearly always helped by milk or an antacid.

A person may have typical symptoms and yet have no ulcer. The diagnosis can be confirmed in an outpatient clinic by an

X-ray examination after drinking a 'barium meal' or by fibre-optic endoscopy in which the doctor examines the inside of the stomach through a flexible telescope.

To the sufferer dyspepsia (indigestion) may seem like an ulcer. The symptoms are feelings of heartburn, distension of the stomach, premature satiety after only a few mouthfuls of food, nausea, and general belly-ache, and yet, if the patient is investigated, no disease is found. Antacids help, but the problem tends to be a recurring one.

Acid appears to play a leading role in the causes of peptic ulcer. The stomach usually produces a strong acid but protects itself from being digested by this acid by secreting a coating of mucus. It is thought that stress may increase the secretion of acid and decrease the secretion of mucus.

Food neutralises gastric acid, and it is during long periods of stressful work on an empty stomach that the acid begins to damage the lining of the stomach, and an ulcer starts. Alcohol, particularly spirits taken on an empty stomach, further damages the mucosa. Smoking probably increases secretion of gastric acid and may interfere with secretion of mucus; it therefore contributes to the formation of ulcers and slows their healing.

Some drugs (most of which are available only on prescription) can cause a peptic ulcer. Aspirin and anti-inflammatory drugs used in the treatment of arthritis are the worst offenders. Aspirin can be bought over the counter, on its own or contained in any one of a large number of patent medicines – some for the relief of dyspepsia. Anyone suffering from dyspepsia should read carefully what is contained in a medicine to make sure that the list of ingredients does not include aspirin. Be warned by 'salicyl . . .' in the name; for instance, sodium salicylate, salicylic acid, acetylsalicylic acid.

An antacid, in liquid or tablet form, relieves pain by neutralising gastric acid. Taken regularly, in sufficient quantities for long enough, an antacid can heal an ulcer. It is, however, surer and more convenient to be prescribed an ulcer-healing drug, of which there are a number. The doctor's choice depends on factors such as the site of the ulcer. A full course of such treatment lasts four to six weeks and almost always heals an ulcer.

Ulcers often return unless the conditions that encouraged the ulcer in the first place are changed. The details of a diet are probably less important than is popularly thought, but it seems sensible to avoid fried, fatty or highly spiced food, and anything which seems to cause pain.

premenstrual tension

Disorders of menstruation such as premenstrual tension can both cause, and be influenced by, stress. During the days before the onset of menstruation, the woman feels physically and mentally fragile, anxious and irritable, and stressful circumstances are coped with less well.

Premenstrual tension describes one symptom of premenstrual syndrome. PMS is a collection of physical and mental symptoms which occur for a few days (even up to a fortnight) before a period and stop when the period begins. It is the timing of the symptoms in each monthly cycle, rather than the symptoms themselves, that determines whether it is likely that the cause is premenstrual syndrome.

The mental symptoms include tension, depression, anxiety or panic attacks, irritability, angry outbursts, crying for no reason, forgetfulness or mental confusion. The physical symptoms might be fatigue, clumsiness, food cravings. Water retention may cause breast tenderness, bloating of the stomach, ankles, feet or fingers and joint pains. Headaches, backache, acne, cold sores, are all indicators if they recur regularly before periods.

Once PMS is recognised by a woman and her doctor, she may find relief from a number of therapies. Some women find relaxation techniques help, also a change in diet. Others may benefit from tranquillisers on the days when anxiety is at its worst. Counselling can help a woman to reorganise her life according to the predictable changes in her well-being.

Ø **The National Association for Premenstrual Syndrome**, 25 Market Street, Guildford, Surrey GU1 4LB (telephone 0483-572715) with a day helpline 0483-572806 and night helpline 09592-4371 entitles members, who pay £6 for twelve months, to receive literature, a list of members, new information relating to PMS and to attend meetings. A network of support groups is being planned.

Ø **Pre-Menstrual Tension Advisory Service**, PO Box 268, Hove, East Sussex BN3 1RW (telephone 0273-771366) provides nutritional advice by post to PMT sufferers (for a fee of £36 for six months). An alternative six-month programme including telephone and letter consultations costs £56.

rheumatoid arthritis

A feature of this disease is a proliferation of inflammatory tissue in the membrane which lines some of the joints of the body, especially the hands and feet, wrists, elbows and ankles. It produces swelling, pain and stiffness of joints and can become disabling.

The specific cause of the inflammatory reaction is not fully clear. It seems likely that the body's immune mechanisms which normally play an important part in the defence of the body against disease are disturbed so that they are activated by some of the body's own protein, producing destruction and inflammation. Research is going on as to whether, how and why the body's immune mechanisms react in this destructive way in rheumatoid arthritis.

There may be a link between stress and the onset of rheumatoid arthritis, but this is difficult to prove. In a recent study, it was found that in the three months before onset of rheumatoid arthritis, the women affected underwent significantly more stressful life events than a control group.

Ø **The Arthritis & Rheumatism Council**, 41 Eagle Street, London WC1R 4AR (telephone 01-405 8572) publishes three times a year the ARC magazine with up-to-date information on research into the cause of rheumatic diseases and the results that are being achieved.

skin diseases

Skin diseases which, although not primarily of emotional origin may to a greater or lesser extent be aggravated or perpetuated by stress, include urticaria (nettle rash or hives); itching without obvious skin disease, often in the anogenital region; acne, especially the type in which picking and squeezing at the lesions perpetuates them and produces the typical excoriated appearance.

Emotional factors and stress are important in the development, aggravation and perpetuation of many skin diseases, and the stress and misery caused by the skin disease may lead to a vicious circle. An awareness by friends, relatives and the general public that skin disease is seldom contagious, that it is not dirty, that it is not the sufferers' fault and that it causes them great embarrassment, would help to reduce the stress caused by skin disease and make the treatment of it easier.

Atopic eczema is a disorder with an inherited tendency towards itchy dry skin, areas of redness and tiny blisters which break to produce crusts. The condition may be associated with asthma or hay fever. Scratching leads to scabs and to thickening of the skin, which in turn leads to further itching. Atopic eczema commonly gets worse at times of emotional stress – for example, when facing exams, entry to a new school, the birth of a sibling.

Ø **National Eczema Society**, Tavistock House North, Tavistock Square, London WC1H 9SR (telephone 01-388 4097) aims to encourage research into eczema and to spread information about it and its management; publishes a quarterly journal, leaflets and information packs; there are nationwide groups which meet for talks and discussions and exchange of information.

Psoriasis tends to run in families. The visible signs may come and go spontaneously; they are red scaly patches, usually affecting the outer surfaces of elbows and knees, the scalp and back, sometimes affecting the nails to produce gross thickening. Various factors may provoke psoriasis, including, in some people, stress. The emotional stress caused by psoriasis is often one of the worst features of the disease.

Ø **The Psoriasis Association**, 7 Milton Street, Northampton NN2 7JG (telephone 0604-711129) is a self-help association which aims to encourage research into psoriasis and to spread information about it; there are local groups providing social contact and mutual aid and support.

tinnitus

This condition, caused by a small abnormality in the hearing nerve, is the sensation of sound (ringing in the ear) without an external stimulus, which can be heard only by the person suffering from it. It affects people with normal hearing as well as those who are hearing-impaired. Many of those who have this distressing condition experience acute stress as a direct consequence of having tinnitus. It is known that stress can trigger it and can cause tinnitus to worsen. It is, therefore, most important that sufferers should be able to reduce stress levels. At the present time there is no cure for tinnitus although tinnitus maskers are proving helpful in alleviating the condition. Research has been carried out into a form of music therapy, using personal stereos, with compositions containing high frequencies.

Ø **The British Tinnitus Association**, 105 Gower Street, London WC1E 6AH (telephone 01-387 8033) publishes a quarterly newsletter which includes details of over 50 local BTA groups.

ANXIETY AND DEPRESSION

The two emotional responses of anxiety and depression are closely related, and are linked to stress, but not necessarily as cause and effect. As a general rule, anxiety tends to be a reaction to stressful threats, and depression a reaction to stressful losses, but many people experience a mixture of the two.

An anxious person is often tense and watchful, as if waiting for information, and may over-react to noise and other stimuli. He may feel in imminent, unidentified danger and unable to communicate this fear. Hope and despair tend to alternate, whereas depression is a prevailing mood of pessimism and discouragement.

The feeling of depression is a sustained mood of sadness and pessimism, despair and despondency. Sadness from time to time is normal and is understandable if things are going wrong or where there is some unhappy episode in the person's life. But, generally, the mood lifts as the person puts the event into perspective. In some people, however, the feelings of depression become much deeper and more upsetting, and out of proportion to the problems in their life.

anxiety

With anxiety may be associated physical symptoms such as sweating, tightness in the chest, a sinking feeling in the stomach, a lightness in the head, possibly dizziness. The person tends to be pale or sometimes, but less often, flushed. He tires quickly, his pulse is rapid and the heart overacting: mild exertion produces an undue increase in pulse rate and respiration rate. Sexual interest tends to be in abeyance. The function of every organ in the body may be affected in some degree.

The anxiety is never far below the surface and affects most aspects of the person's existence with a fear, often irrational, of the unknown, and anticipation of imminent catastrophe. Because the person's anxiety threshold is low, quite trivial events may be perceived as stressful. Thus, the breakdown of a domestic appliance may be magnified by an anxious housewife into a major crisis. Or an anxious man may worry over his possible workload when he reads that the company he works for is increasing its dividend to shareholders.

Many anxieties are normal in the sense that almost everyone experiences them – for example, going to the dentist, taking an important examination or being interviewed. Sometimes the anxiety is a reaction to very real stresses and threats: money difficulties, family problems or looming unemployment. Most people manage fairly well and do not experience undue anxiety unless the stresses in their life become too great.

abnormal anxiety states

It is only when the anxiety is so severe, pervasive and persistent that it colours the person's every thought and feeling that it is no longer normal but becomes an illness, or when worries about stupid little things become exaggerated out of proportion, that the anxiety is abnormal.

Anxiety can become an overwhelming sense of foreboding of something terrible about to happen. The worries are ever-present; the sufferer wakes up to what he feels will be a day of problems, and goes to bed with them still unresolved and preying on his mind. Stresses become more intense as the person becomes more anxious, until the unfortunate individual is in danger of reacting to almost everything in his life with foreboding, tension and sometimes, in severe instances, with sheer terror.

The heavy sense of dread is more intolerable because of its vagueness. The anxiety is so upsetting that the sufferer becomes irritable and snappy. Anxiety interferes with attention and concentration; work, especially intricate tasks, becomes difficult. The person may feel peculiarly detached from reality as if he were looking down on himself: trying to become detached from stressful reality is a protective mechanism.

Anxiety states also produce bodily symptoms similar to physical stress responses. A feeling that the heart is about to stop, giddiness, faintness and unsteadiness may occur, so may chest pain, difficulty in swallowing and a feeling of a lump in the throat, tension headache and various aches and pains.

panic

Many sufferers from anxiety experience panic attacks. These are acute episodes of extreme anxiety which the sufferer finds uncontrollable. Bodily symptoms such as palpitations, faintness and sweating are intensified (which in itself is frightening). Other symptoms include inability to breathe or over-breathing, nausea, vomiting, belching, urgent calls to pass urine or stools, diarrhoea, trembling.

The panic attacks may come on for no apparent reason, or be related to a phobic situation or object.

phobias

By definition, phobia is an irrational fear that is out of proportion to the particular situation. Some people are made greatly anxious in certain situations or when confronted by certain objects. A common form of this is agoraphobia, a fear of crowds and public places. The sufferer is unable to leave the house on his (or more commonly her) own, cannot travel on public transport, or go into crowded shops without becoming panicky. Agoraphobia may strike out of the blue or, for many people, is the aftermath of a period of a great stress such as illness or bereavement, its onset being part of a delayed reaction to such an event.

Fear of objects can include dogs, birds and snakes. A person afraid of spiders may not only refuse to live in the country but refuse to live in a ground-floor flat in town. Or a person with a fear of lifts would be prepared to walk up endless flights of stairs.

Even when the sufferer fully realises that his fears are irrational, these situations become extremely stressful. The person should seek medical and psychological help if the phobia is getting steadily worse or is interfering with daily activities. A short course of treatment aimed specifically at helping with the phobia can be very effective. The first step is to see the general practitioner.

Ø **The Open Door Association**, c/o 447 Pensby Road, Heswall, Wirral, Merseyside L61 9PQ is a self-help organisation offering an information service. Members receive an information sheet on self-help and the offer of a book *Conquering Your Agoraphobia* (£4.50).

Ø **The Phobics Society**, 4 Cheltenham Road, Chorlton-cum-Hardy, Manchester M21 1QN (telephone 061-881 1937) teaches sufferers to understand and cope with their phobia and helps them to lead a happier and constructive life.

abnormal depressive states

When a depressive state develops, this may be clearly related to an adverse life event or an event which has given rise to a feeling of loss or disappointment – such as bereavement, unemployment, divorce, or surgery to remove part of the body. Initial despair at such experiences is understandable, but it should lift gradually. If, instead, it pervades the person's whole life, it is an abnormal depressive state: the depression seems to be an over-reaction and is a type of illness, which may stem largely from the person's personality.

In other instances, people suffer a depression which is completely unexplained, seemingly coming 'out of the blue'.

The depression may appear, perhaps gradually, with no obvious stressful incident preceding it. However, it is now thought that even these 'out of the blue' depressive states may be triggered by events which the sufferer has found stressful.

post-natal depression

When a depressive state develops after the birth of a baby, it is called post-natal depression. This is not the brief weepy period three or four days after the birth ('baby blues' possibly associated with hormonal changes) which many women experience, but sets in some weeks after the birth. The cause of post-natal depression is not agreed, but the stress of giving birth and looking after a baby could trigger off a depressive state in a woman predisposed to react to stress in this way.

depressive illness

There are both emotional and physical aspects of depressive states, but not every sufferer experiences them all.

The prime psychological symptom is a lowering of mood with a persistent and prevailing sadness. The person's whole life is darkened. He or she cannot enjoy life; former interests and hobbies are neglected. Family and friends, who try to help, are rejected. Sufferers stop making an effort with their personal appearance, they cannot concentrate and their memory worsens. They may be irritable, and elderly sufferers in particular may be agitated. An 'agitated depression' is a form of depressive illness in which a depressed mood is absent.

The person may feel his life to be worthless and unfulfilled. Small mistakes are magnified into major transgressions, he feels inferior, undeserving of help or gratitude and often blames himself for his predicament.

Physical pain such as headache, backache and shooting pains in the face and neck may develop. People who had pains before they had any depressive episodes, find that the pains become worse. Hypochondria is sometimes a feature of a

he cannot sleep properly & suffers loss of appetite + loss of libido or sex drive

depressive state: for example, the sufferer may, quite wrongly, believe that he has cancer.

It may well be difficult for the person to get to sleep, and he or she might then wake very early feeling particularly depressed. Some depressed people, usually younger ones, tend to oversleep rather than suffer from insomnia. Constipation is common: many sufferers lose their appetite, and thus lose some weight, sometimes quite dramatically. There is often a loss of libido or sex drive.

A combined state of anxiety and depression is quite common. Some sufferers drink heavily, though this only makes them feel more depressed.

anti-depressants

There is anti-depressant drug therapy for depressive illness. Anti-depressant drugs are prescribed to correct a biochemical imbalance in the brain. The onset of effect is slow, taking ten to fourteen days; after that, the majority of patients respond to a short course of treatment lasting usually six to eight weeks. This is particularly important in prevention of suicide.

While physical factors play a part in many cases of depression only some doctors (and patients) believe that people who respond to personal stress and strain by becoming depressed suffer from chemical disturbances and imbalances in the brain.

∅ **MIND (National Association for Mental Health)**, 22 Harley Street, London W1N 2ED (telephone 01-637 0741) has published a special report on "Anti-depressants" including the trade-names of the drugs, dosage and side-effects. (MIND has local affiliated associations throughout England and Wales. Some can offer help through information/advice services or support groups. Head office can give information, literature and referral to a local association.)

People who are prescribed anti-depressants are warned to be

very careful about taking some other preparations, for example, antihistamines, certain drugs to reduce blood pressure, appetite suppressants, alcohol.

It is possible for a doctor to prescribe tablets which combine the actions of anti-depressants and tranquillisers (anti anxiety agents), but this is generally not recommended because of the side effects.

minor tranquillisers

These are not mini versions of so-called major tranquillisers prescribed for severe mental illness, but sedatives.

Currently, the most widely prescribed drugs in this group are the benzodiazepines such as diazepam (Valium), chlordiazepoxide (Librium) and lorazepam (Ativan) during the day, and nitrazepam (Mogadon) or tenazepam at night. They calm people down and make them more able to cope and make their problems seem less insistent.

However, taking tranquillisers for stress reactions does not of itself deal with the stress. If a patient goes to the doctor with a stress response that is caused by a problem and is treated with tranquillisers, the problem is merely shelved, not solved. In many cases, the person will eventually have to do more than just take drugs.

It is now generally agreed that tranquillisers will cease being effective after a few weeks' continuous use.

Tranquillisers are not free of drawbacks. They may cause some drowsiness and can dull sensitivities and, after prolonged dosage, lessen intellectual capabilities. It is now clear that the benzodiazepines – tranquillisers and sleeping pills – cause dependence. People who have taken benzodiazepines for six weeks or more experience unpleasant withdrawal symptoms when they try to stop their drug.

In the summer of 1987, the Consumers' Association's *Drug and Therapeutics Bulletin* said that there are other ways of dealing with anxiety and tension than prescribing tranquillisers. GPs are developing their skills of managing anxious patients without drugs.

However, in cases where anxiety is excessive and disabling, short-term use of tranquillisers may help the person, as long as the risk of dependence is avoided if the relief helps the person to resume a normal occupational, social and marital life.

If the drug is discontinued gradually and under medical supervision, withdrawal symptoms can be much less nasty.

Ø **TRANX (UK) Ltd (National Tranquilliser Advice Centre)**, 25a Masons Avenue, Wealdstone, Harrow HA3 5AH (telephone 01-427 2065) offers self-help groups for people who want to overcome their addiction to minor tranquillisers and sleeping pills; provides one-to-one counselling; advice and information concerning withdrawal symptoms.

Ø **Accept**, Accept/Drugs Helpline (telephone 01-286 3339) provides free and confidential advice, counselling and day treatment for hard drugs. Accept Publications has a wide range of low-cost literature on addictions including *Survival Skills* for abstinence, *Drinkwatchers Handbook* for sensible drinking, *Action on Tranquillisers* for coping with pills. There is multilingual counselling for ethnic minorities (01-577 6059).

drug dependence

In some people, the relaxation and escape from stress through drugs leads them to repeat their initial drug 'high'. (For some addicts, the feeling of belonging to, and being accepted by, a sub-culture of other addicts is an important factor perpetuating their habit.) Eventually, when psychological or physical dependence has become established, the habit may be maintained partly because of the wish to induce a drugged state but also, in the case of opium-like compounds, to prevent withdrawal symptoms. The need to procure further drug supplies is a further major stress dominating the addict's life.

Drug taking is often kept secret. In some cases, there may be very little objective evidence, especially in the early stages, unless someone happens to see the person at a time when he is actually under the influence of the drug or in a disturbed condition. If a person can admit that he has a drug problem, his general practitioner can refer him to the local psychiatric clinic or, in some localities, to a specialised clinic, generally called an addiction centre or drug dependence clinic or drug dependency unit or detoxification unit. Some centres also accept self-referral, without having to go to a general practitioner first.

In some cases, the person will be offered admission to hospital where the drugs will be gradually withdrawn and other drugs given to alleviate the withdrawal distress. The process takes up to a few weeks and during that time the person's general state of health, which may be poor, will also receive attention. In some centres, attempts at withdrawal on an outpatient or daypatient basis are made.

In many cases, withdrawal from the drug is only the first stage, followed by longer-term rehabilitation at a special centre, or in hospital, where some of the underlying problems that lead to drug abuse are treated.

Ø **Standing Conference on Drug Abuse**, (SCODA), 1–4 Hatton Place, Hatton Garden, London EC1N 8ND (telephone 01-430 2341) is the national co-ordinating body for voluntary organisations and agencies working in the drugs field. Regional workers keep in touch with developments and a newsletter is published on a regular basis.

You can call **Freephone Drug Problems** (dial 100 for the operator and ask for Freephone Drug Problems) and you will hear a recorded message giving telephone contact numbers for counties in England. In Scotland, ring the Scottish Drugs Forum on 041-221 1175. In Wales ring the All Wales Drugsline on 0222-383313. In Northern Ireland, ring the Northern Ireland Regional Unit on 0232-229808 (24 hours). If you cannot find a local service write to SCODA.

Ø **Institute for the Study of Drug Dependence** at the same address (telephone 01-430 1901) gives information on all aspects of non-medical use of drugs and on the risk of dependence attaching to drugs. It can also advise on risks and side effects of drugs and on their legal status. It cannot offer individual help or counselling.

Ø **South Wales Association for the Prevention of Addiction**, 1 Neville Street, Cardiff CF1 8LP (telephone 0222-383313) offers a 24 hour helpline telephone counselling service plus 12 local drop-in centres and group sessions in South and Mid Glamorgan. Drug awareness weeks can be arranged, and there is a quarterly newsletter.

Ø **Release**, 169 Commercial Street, London E1 6BW (telephone 01-377 5905 or 24 hour service 01-603 8654) is a national advice, information and referral agency dealing with drugs and criminal legal problems, and drugs law problems. Drug advice service covers both prescribed and illegal drug use.

Ø **Narcotics Anonymous**, PO Box 417, London SW10 0DP (telephone 01-351 6794/6066) is a fellowship of people recovering from addiction, following a recovery programme along the lines of Alcoholics Anonymous.

Ø **Families Anonymous**, 5–7 Parsons Green, London SW6 4UL (telephone 01-731 8060) is a self-help organisation for the families and friends of drug abusers (based on the principles of Alcoholics Anonymous). Arranges weekly discussion meetings.

effects on others

Coping with a chronically depressed man, with some risk of suicide, may tax the resources of the most patient of wives. Mental illness produces stresses not only on the patient but also on his relatives. For example, living with a schizophrenic person is notoriously stressful because of his or her bizarre behaviour and unpredictability. A house-bound phobic house-wife may put great stress on her husband who has to do all the shopping and take time off work to stay with her if her panics become extreme. If the person who is suffering from psychiatric illness gets medical help, the benefit should extend to the patient's partner.

Ø **Fellowship of Depressives Anonymous**, 36 Chestnut Avenue, Beverley, North Humberside HU17 9QU is a national organisation which brings depressives together for support and encouragement. Facilities for members include a quarterly newsletter, penfriend scheme, book list. Information is available about local SDA groups; open meetings are held every two months at various places which anyone interested in depression and its problems may attend.

Ø **Depressives Associated**, PO Box 5, Castle Town, Portland, Dorset DT5 1BQ provides information, support and understanding for people who suffer with depression and for relatives who want to help. For information write, enclosing a 9 × 6 in stamped addressed envelope.

suicide

People who are depressed may experience suicidal feelings. Usually, unless very socially isolated, they communicate their intentions – however obliquely – to others. Warnings of this sort must be taken seriously. It is quite erroneous to suppose that people who talk about suicide never attempt it. But a person suffering from depression does not necessarily have suicidal thoughts and if he does not bring up the subject, there is no need for you to do so.

People who attempt suicide have often experienced a major increase in stress, such as a recent breakdown in relationships, or other recent significant life events. In the elderly, physical factors such as pain and cancer may lead to suicide.

help from others

A person who feels suicidal should try to discuss it with someone and, if possible, get skilled medical advice and ask to be referred to a psychiatrist. At the very least, he or she should confide in a friend, or phone the Samaritans. Talking about suicide to a sympathetic person makes it less likely.

If you are a friend who is being confided in, take it seriously: people who threaten to kill themselves are quite likely to try to carry out their threat. Try to persuade the person to see his or her general practitioner. As a last resort, do so yourself or communicate your concern about the potential suicide to close relatives of that person.

self-harm

A related but separate problem is deliberate self-harm, attempted suicide, commonly by poisoning. Wrist-slashing is a form of self-destructive behaviour precipitated by stress. It is often carried out by disturbed adolescent girls or young women. In young people who try self-injury, the act may be a protest at the treatment by someone close (such as an unfaithful spouse) or an attempt to draw attention to their own situation and distress. The attempts at self-harm may be half-hearted, leading to severe scarring rather than death.

It is possible for a distant observer to interpret the whole thing as a way of drawing attention to themselves, but only a small minority of people who attempt suicide have this in mind. Most of them live distressing lives, and have been brought to a point of total despair when they just cannot cope.

The person should be persuaded to see the doctor and seek specialist help from a psychiatrist or a clinical psychologist.

Ø the Samaritans

The Samaritans offer a befriending service for the despairing and suicidal. It is primarily a telephone service, but people needing help can also call in person at one of the branches. Telephone callers who seem likely to benefit by meeting a Samaritan face to face are invited to call in. Samaritans may arrange to meet clients away from the centre during the hours when the centre is not open for face-to-face talking. The Samaritans have around 180 centres, manned by volunteers.

The overriding aim is to reduce the number of suicides. The Samaritans are anxious to induce young people to get in touch with them instead of making an attempt at suicide or self-injury; they are also trying to find ways of making it more likely that people who have been admitted to hospital after attempting suicide will, on discharge, turn to them for help. They are also concerned that the elderly, who are a high-risk age group, should be aware of their services and avail themselves of them.

If a caller is concerned about another person, the Samaritans try to support him in his anxiety and to suggest ways of obtaining help for his friend. The Samaritans do not intrude upon people who have not sought their help directly, unless an identified responsible person informs them of the need of someone who is too young or old or ill to ask in person, in which case they may make a tentative offer of help.

The local telephone number can be found in the phone book. It is usually an easily remembered local number and often prominently advertised.

GENERAL PRACTITIONER –AND TEAM

The general practitioner should be the first, rather than the last, resort of the distressed. A doctor has to deal with all aspects of human living which impinge on health.

Many GPs work in a group practice and are part of a team. In a good family practice, the patient may get help from a health visitor and district nurse to help with social problems, a physiotherapist who can advise on relaxation, a receptionist who knows the local set-up, a practice nurse. Practice nurses are experienced human beings who know what life is all about and are great stress-relievers. There may be a voluntary counsellor within the practice with whom people might have two or three sessions a week to talk over problems.

Doctors vary widely in their attitude to their patients' stress responses and minor mental illness, from the sympathetic listener to the provider of medication.

Tranquillisers should not be prescribed as a routine, but may be used in the short term, if the anxiety response is severe. Sometimes an anti-depressant drug can be helpful if the depression is well-established. But minor stress responses usually resolve without drugs. Sometimes the doctor just has to point out that the youngest children can go to a creche, and that the health visitor will organise this, for the stress responses in the stressed mother to resolve themselves. She might not have thought of the solution for herself, or known how to set about it.

There is much less need for prescribing tranquillisers if the doctor believes in talking to his patients, or refers them to someone skilled in counselling. Part of what is called family medicine is talking and listening. Nowadays, a patient should not have to fear being told to "pull yourself together".

GPs nowadays have more time because of the appointments

system, and counselling is taught not only at medical school but at post-graduate training.

The doctor, taking a proper history of the symptoms can, in itself, be reassuring and can help to put both the symptoms and the stress which produces them into perspective. In some cases, just the GP putting his stethoscope on the patient will relieve the pain.

If you have a general practitioner who will not listen, or of whom – or whose receptionist – you are afraid or feel ill at ease with, go and find another. The *Which?* report in May 1987 explains that you need either to get your old doctor to agree and sign your medical card, or you have to send the card off to the family practitioner committee so they can authorise a change. Either way, you need to find a new doctor who is prepared to accept you as a patient.

phone-in

Healthline provides an extensive library of taped messages lasting from two to six minutes about medical and health problems, including stress, acute anxiety and depression. The tapes have been written and approved by medical experts and most give details of useful organisations as well as telling you more about the particular subject.

The service is confidential and is free, apart from the cost of your telephone call. Dial 01-980 4848 between 2 p.m. and 10 p.m. any day of the week. An operator will answer and play the tape of your choice.

The Healthline directory which lists all the tapes available can be obtained from Box 499, London E2 9PU.

(Healthline should not be confused with Healthcall, which offers a similar service but for which the British Telecom's 'M' rate, which is considerably higher, is charged.)

physical checks and diagnoses

Many doctors prefer not to over-investigate complaints in a person who seems to be going through a period of stress. But if any special tests are needed, for example to make sure there is no heart trouble, the doctor or hospital will carry them out.

Reassurance that there is nothing physically wrong is powerful in reducing the additional stress which worrying about the symptoms can produce. Reassurance does not mean that the doctor suspects the patient of fabricating his symptoms; he may be able to tell that the organ producing the symptom is not impaired. For instance, the heart beat may be irregular without the heart being diseased.

However, if in conditions such as high blood pressure or rheumatoid arthritis, stress has resulted in longer-term changes, treatment rather than just reassurance will be needed to try to remedy changes that have taken place.

The classification of diseases that doctors, particularly GPs, can use in recording their patients' diseases and problems has recently been expanded to give greater precision to diagnoses and to enable life events to be recorded. It is increasingly being recognised that illness can follow such events.

alternative and complementary therapies

A criticism of conventional medicine is that it encourages people to rely on cures rather than to understand, and take some responsibility for, the causes of their ill health. Wonder treatments such as antibiotics, cortisone, anti-depressant drugs and intricate heart surgery have helped foster this view. Diagnosis and treatment in alternative medicine are aimed not so much at relieving symptoms as at finding and correcting ways in which the body is in conflict with its environment.

Alternative (or complementary) therapy covers many different therapies which can be used in place of (alternatively to) or alongside (complementary to) conventional or orthodox medicine. These 'traditional' techniques which are helpful in the healing process include acupuncture, music therapy, therapeutic massage, biofeedback, colour therapy, exercise, diet, laying on of hands.

Critics of alternative therapies say that they work by a placebo effect, and that it is only the practitioner's interest in the patient, during generally long consultations, and his assurances that the treatment works, which cause the patient to get better. To some extent, this is what happens with conventional treatments, too.

Holistic medicine uses alternative techniques as well as conventional medicine as part of the whole healing process. The conventional approach takes less account than the holistic of psychosocial and occupational stress, personality and behaviour factors. The holistic approach brings these factors to the awareness of the individual as well as teaching coping skills through relaxation, meditation and stress management.

∅ **The British Holistic Medical Association**, 179 Gloucester Place, London NW1 6DX (telephone 01-262 5299) was set up by doctors and medical students interested in the whole-person approach to healthcare. Holism was understood to rest on the principle of responding to a person as a whole within the environment, seeing that person as mind, body and spirit; to be willing to consider a wide range of interventions (including orthodox drugs and surgery, education and communication skills, self-help techniques and complementary therapies). The BHMA organises regional and nation-wide conferences, workshops and lectures and sells tapes dealing with self-help through a variety of methods ranging from relieving anxiety without drugs to healthy eating.

Ø **The British Medical Acupuncture Society**, 67–69 Chancery Lane, London WC2A 1AS has a register of doctors who use acupuncture in their practice and will send a list of the names and addresses (for £1).

Ø **The Council for Acupuncture**, Suite 1, 19a Cavendish Square, London W1M 9AD have a register of non-medically qualified acupuncturists – most of these practice traditional acupuncture.

Ø **The National Institute of Medical Herbalists**, c/o 41 Hatherly Road, Winchester, Hants SO22 6RR can send you the list of about 160 registered non-medically qualified medical herbalists in Britain (send SAE).

The *Which?* report on complementary medicine, "Magic or Medicine?" in October 1986 recommended that 'If you want to see a practitioner it would be a good idea to ask friends, family and your GP for a recommendation. But you should also try to ensure that the practitioner has been properly trained. At the moment, the only thing you can do is to select someone who is registered with one of the professional organisations which insists on its members having undergone training to a specified standard.'

It is likely that if you consult someone practising alternative medicine he will enquire fully into how you live and will put emphasis on adjusting your lifestyle.

People who are interested in any forms of alternative therapy should not feel shy of trying out methods which they think may suit them. It would be a mistake to think that any one system of treatment is the answer to all human disorders; most of us can benefit by selecting appropriate bits from different methods.

HELP FROM OTHERS

Talking over problems and sharing one's worries is one of the most useful and positive steps to lessen stress. Sometimes just putting fears or emotions into words makes them clearer and more easy to come to terms with, or makes it possible to see difficulties in their proper perspective.

Someone who would be the right confidant for one situation may be inappropriate or even disastrous in other circumstances. For difficulties at work, a spouse may be ideal to discuss things with; but a wife who has consistently undervalued her husband's abilities is not going to be much use in discussing dispassionately his feeling of failure at being passed over for promotion. Conversely, if she has always regarded him as unfairly held back in the promotion stakes, she may add to his sense of grievance, just or unjust, and not help an objective assessment of the present difficulty.

who is a confidant
The more neutral the person, the more useful. There must be mutual faith and trust, and honesty rather than play-acting. In general, the role of a confidant is less that of giving advice than of letting the other person talk and offload some of the worries; solving the problems is only incidental. Some people have the knack of just allowing a stressed person to talk, hardly intervening except for an encouraging word, or nod to continue.

Marital problems are particularly difficult to discuss. If you can do so, without feelings of disloyalty, it may be better to talk to someone other than the partner, at least to begin with. Marriage guidance counsellors can help with relationship and sometimes sexual problems; many general practitioners (or someone in their team) offer psychosexual counselling.

Close friends can be useful in discussing general problems and sometimes there can be a reciprocal give-and-take of help and advice. However, one must be aware of the barrack-room lawyer, or the instant pundit or the self-styled expert, always ready to take over the lives of others. If specialised legal, financial or medical matters appear to be involved, it is better to seek the advice of a lawyer, accountant, bank manager, or doctor. The citizens advice bureau is staffed by people experienced in giving practical advice and in sorting out problems in any particular case.

Some people are delegated to act as counsellors as part of their job. Personnel officers employed by large companies, although not primarily there to help people who feel stressed, can be useful confidants. They are also able to help in practical ways, especially if the stress stems from work situations.

counselling

Counselling can help people to identify their sources of stress by putting into words their fears and anxieties and then to adjust to them, or else to adjust their circumstances. Some people go to a friend or confidant, but many prefer the anonymity of an independent counsellor.

Counsellors are trained to be available to listen, and by being empathetic but not identifying too closely with the 'client' can sometimes mirror back the problem and increase the person's understanding of it. They help the client to sort out the main difficulties and identify the trouble spots and work out possible ways of coping or overcoming them himself. Counselling is not about advising, as it is sometimes mistakenly perceived, nor should it be threatening because the counsellor is totally non-judgmental and confidentiality is paramount. During a crisis, a counsellor can sometimes help to identify a new approach which can be used as a starting point in the new life style.

who does the counselling

The doctor may find himself in the role of confidant, especially where the stressed person has developed worrying bodily symptoms for which he seeks reassurance and relief. He may focus on the symptoms, play down the general stress problems and prescribe tranquillisers. But many doctors are now trained to act as counsellors and, unless under too much pressure themselves, will assume what may be regarded as a non-medical role. Studies carried out to assess how effective counselling can be have shown that even quite brief counselling for a few sessions helped to lessen anxiety as effectively as tranquillisers.

Traditionally, ministers of religion are delegated by society to deal with the problems of their fellow men. Clergymen themselves have been known to suffer severely from the strain of other people's problems and to need stress counselling themselves. Fewer people profess themselves to belong to any organised religious body, so not many people avail themselves of this source of help.

Some people want immediate support and can obtain this from 'phone-in counselling. In a severe crisis, for example, there are the Samaritans. The Mental Health Foundation publishes *Someone to talk to*, a directory of self-help and community support agencies in the UK (including some 'phone-in services) which is distributed to libraries, advice centres, health and social services agencies.

Ø **Westminster Pastoral Foundation**, 23 Kensington Square, London W8 5HN (telephone 01-937 6956) has a network of counselling centres covering most areas of the country which offer a range of counselling services, including individual, group, marital and family counselling. The most appropriate service for each person is assessed with them at their first session. Those who seek help are expected to contribute financially as their means allow but no one is denied help if they cannot pay.

Ø **The British Association for Counselling**, 37a Sheep Street, Rugby, Warwickshire CV21 3BX (telephone 0788-78328) can supply information about counselling services nationally, and about individual counsellors in private practice who are members of the Association.

The following is based on, and in part taken from, information sheets published by the British Association for Counselling.

GUIDELINES FOR THOSE SEEKING COUNSELLING

"Whoever you are, whatever your age, whatever the situation or problem which you are facing; whether you are worried, depressed, confused, feeling bad about yourself, wanting to make some changes in your life or coping with unwanted change or crisis, it can help to talk things over, in confidence, with an understanding outsider. Good, objective listening is the basis of all counselling. Some counsellors specialise in particular concerns (e.g. marital, sexual, bereavement, educational, vocational) but many are generalist counsellors who regard it as part of their counselling to help you to consider all aspects of your situation and all the possible sources of help.

This kind of talking about what is on your mind can help you to discover more about yourself, your strengths and weaknesses, values and priorities and not only to find your own solutions but also to carry them out; to take some action for yourself. You can expect a good counsellor to respect you and not to impose opinions on you nor make decisions for you. Do not expect to be told what to do. Good counselling is essentially a lively, human, personal and mutual exchange between two people; it is a process which requires commitments of time and effort by both parties, though the number of meetings needed will vary with individual circumstances. The aim is to help you to find your own answers and to become more in charge of your life rather than less so. It is quite different from other kinds of help in which you become, appropriately at times, the object of diagnosis or assessment and are then told what to do. In some more specialised forms of counselling, however, the counsellor may decide to give you some very definite instructions to help you overcome a specific difficulty, but only after you have together explored your situation very thoroughly and both agreed on a particular course of action.

One of the aims of counselling is to help you if you are confused, so you do not have to be clear as to what your problem is, or indeed, as to whether you have one or not. A good counsellor will help you to overcome any difficulties you may have in expressing yourself and will accept that you may need to modify what you say, not just once, but repeatedly until you feel you have got it right. It can, however, sometimes help you to find the right kind of counselling and to make the best use of the first session, if you think about the following questions:

○ What is wrong?
○ How long has this been going on?
○ How widely does this affect my life?
○ Is it about feelings or actions, or both?
○ Does it involve others who might also want or need counselling?
○ What do I hope the result of counselling will be? . . .

The first meeting with a counsellor is usually an opportunity to discuss whether continued counselling would be appropriate to your needs and is without obligation on either side. At some stage you need to ask about practical things such as time, place, cost and duration of meetings. Feel free to ask any questions you wish, as you need to know where you stand, and to satisfy yourself that this is a person whom you feel able to trust and with whom you would like to work. Be prepared to give as complete and honest a picture of your circumstances as you can, so that together you can decide whether what the counsellor can offer will match your needs. If you decide that counselling is not going to be right for you, it does not mean that there is necessarily something wrong with you. It may be that another counsellor would be more suitable, or that you need a different kind of help.

Counselling sometimes makes you feel worse before you feel better. It can involve talking about painful things. However, unless you feel strongly that the counselling which you receive is completely wrong for you, do give it a chance to work. Just as you would not be hasty about entering into counselling, do not be hasty in withdrawing from it. It is difficult to judge your own progress, but at the very least, if you feel that you are communicating, are really in touch with each other (and this may take more than one meeting) something worthwhile is taking place. If, after several meetings, you do not feel that this is so, it would be best to be honest and say so. You can then discuss whether to continue for an agreed but limited number of meetings and then to review the situation, or you can discuss other sources of help.

It is not always easy to get information about where to go for counselling. The British Association for Counselling can sometimes supply information about counselling services and specialist organisations; it also publishes a directory of counsellors in private practice. Local counselling organisations can usually be traced through your local library, citizens advice bureau, council for voluntary service or doctor's surgery. Local marriage guidance councils can often supply information even if they are unable to offer you appropriate help themselves."

The following is an extract from The British Association for Counselling's information sheet *What is counselling?*

"Counselling occurs when a counsellor meets with a client in a private and confidential setting to explore a difficulty the client is having, distress he may be experiencing or perhaps his dissatisfaction with life or loss of a sense of direction or purpose. It is always at the request of the client and no-one can properly be 'sent' for counselling.

In the counselling sessions the client is enabled, by a person who neither judges nor offers advice, to explore various aspects of his life and his feelings concerning them, by talking about them freely and openly in a way that is rarely possible with friends or family. The counsellor will encourage the expression of feelings and will accept them without becoming burdened by them. Bottled-up feelings such as anger, anxiety, grief and embarrassment can become very intense; an opportunity to express them and talk about them in a secure place can help dissolve them, making them easier to understand and can reduce the pain caused by them.

The relationship between the client and the counsellor is an essential part of the process. As trust is built up, the counsellor will encourage the client to look at aspects of his life, his relationships and himself that he may not have thought of or felt able to face before. Counselling employs some psychological techniques. There may be some exploration of early relationships to discover how he has come to react to certain people or situations in ways that contribute to his difficulties. The counsellor may set out the options open to the client and help him to follow whichever one he chooses. She may help the client to examine the detail of the situations or behaviour which are proving troublesome and to find a small but crucial point which could be changed as a start. Whatever approach the counsellor uses, the client has to make his own choices, to make his own decisions and to put them into action himself.

Counselling may end after a few sessions (sometimes even a single session gives sufficient help) or it may continue over several weeks or many months. Some counsellors specialise in particular areas, such as problems related to alcohol or to debt or to sexual matters. They may give information and advice based on their specialist knowledge and training but in so far as they are counsellors, they will not do so in the context of the counselling relationship.

psychotherapy

The distinction between counselling and psychotherapy is not a matter which need greatly concern anyone seeking help. Most practitioners of either activity, before any commitment on either side is made, will want to be sure that the help they can offer is appropriate for the individual concerned.

There is considerable overlap between counselling and psychotherapy in that much psychotherapy is about overcoming personal difficulties and facilitating change. The methods used in psychotherapy are similar and in some instances identical to those used in counselling."

Psychotherapy may be on an individual or group basis. The main disadvantage of group psychotherapy is that individual problems cannot be discussed in confidence. The advantage is that the members of the group can give each other support and advice – and it is economic of professional time.

Psychotherapy tends to be more intensive and more prolonged and is intended to uncover some of the symbolic transactions which are producing inappropriate responses, such as an adult reacting to another person as if he were still a four-year old reacting to his parent.

A psychotherapist working in a hospital is likely to be more concerned with severe psychological disorders than with the wider range of problems and predicaments about which it is appropriate to consult a counsellor. In private practice, however, a psychotherapist is more likely to accept clients whose need is less severe. Similarly, in private practice, a counsellor's work will overlap that of a psychotherapist. Counsellors who work for voluntary agencies usually concentrate more on the 'everyday' problems and difficulties of life than on severe psychological disorders, though many are qualified to offer, and do in fact engage in, therapeutic work which in any other context would be called psychotherapy. Both psychotherapists and counsellors can help to decide whether to seek further medical or psychiatric advice. Normally they are able to make referrals to appropriate specialists, though frequently this can only be done in consultation with the person's own general practitioner.

The most intensive form of psychotherapy, namely psychoanalysis, involves 4 or 5 hourly sessions a week for a year or more and is the province of highly specialised practitioners, medical and non-medical, who have undergone prolonged training.

During psychoanalysis, the patient recalls with his therapist earlier key relationships. In this way, disordered behaviour patterns which are self-destructive or inappropriate, and which generate misery, can be identified and gradually corrected as the person becomes conscious of them. A dazzling, single discovery of 'the cause of all the trouble' is very unlikely, and is not the aim even though this popular misconception is remarkably persistent.

HELPING ONESELF

Ways of reducing stress can include changing oneself or one's relationships, changing one's activities and one's attitudes, leading a healthier life. Many of these changes will interact; for instance, change of attitude is likely to change one's relationships with others. No simple measure is likely to be an immediate cure-all which will lead to a state of blissful happiness, nor, however, should any measures be thought futile without giving them a chance. Removing even a minor problem can alleviate stress quite suddenly, leaving the person in a better position to cope with major problems.

It is better to make learning to cope with stress a gradual, planned process, rather than a one-off enthusiasm or an obsession which itself becomes a stress.

personality factors

An individual's personality not only affects his perception of external stresses and can even be a source of stress in its own right, it also influences his way of coping with stress.

Personality traits affect people's choice of confidant, how they articulate the problem, how receptive they are to suggestions, to what extent they are able to view the problem dispassionately, and so on.

Personality is a complex aspect of a person's functioning. It is possible to highlight the predominant features of some personality traits, such as anxious, aggressive, inadequate, obsessional, and so on; however, this is inevitably an over-simplification, because most people have a mixture of personality characteristics.

Anxious people may feel reluctant to discuss their problems and may prefer to sweat it out (often literally) on their own. Once the initial resistance is overcome, however, and they find they have a sympathetic listener, they benefit greatly from reassurance.

Obsessional people may chew over their problems ad nauseam and it is only a very patient listener who does not become bored with their constant preoccupations. They are helped by listing their problems in order of priority because their personality makes them give every stressful circumstance equal weight.

The personality trait of obsessionality is closely related to the anxious personality. The person fixes an idea into his mind and mulls over it to the exclusion of other things. External stresses will be magnified several fold because of the continuing ruminations. The person may be constantly checking things such as gas-taps being turned off or windows locked. In general, obsessional traits show themselves as excessive tidiness, inability to see the wood for the trees, over-attention to detail and illogical, often time-wasting strategies for doing things. In extreme cases, people may develop rituals such as washing their hands seven times before each meal; or specific fears, for instance of harming other people.

Introspective individuals may not mull over matters in such an obsessional way, but every event is pondered, both for its implications and for its emotional and intellectual impact. Every activity of life becomes intellectualised and stress can become magnified by concentrating on its potential impact. Introspective people talk about their problems very clearly and with insight. They tend to welcome a listener because they find that the more they agonise over a problem on their own, the more indecisive and confused they become.

A related but different personality trait is that of the *dreamy* individual who elaborates events into a rich imaginary life. This can lessen stress by insulating the person and creating a positive sense of security (a better feeling of security is, however, created by close relationships with others).

The *withdrawn* personality shows a more extreme version of this trait: he has opted out and avoids stress by refusing to allow it to impinge on him. He is protected by his detachment, and by his minimal involvement in life. Such withdrawal may follow a stressful experience as an attempt to cope with it. The really withdrawn and dreamy individuals find talking to other people difficult and may feel that it is impossible to communicate properly.

The *paranoid* individual is guarded and suspicious and sees danger lurking around every corner. He may be touchy and irritable about things, but the stresses are often imagined or exaggerated. Relationships with other people are strained and this is usually the main source of stress; he tries to reduce stress by blaming others.

To a paranoid person, who is prickly and hostile, any attempt to help may seem a threat, any refusal to help a rejection. Great patience and perseverance are needed until the sufferer begins to trust someone.

The *passive*, rather inadequate, person shows another personality trait. Instead of withdrawing from stressful experiences, the individual allows them to wash over him like waves on the seashore. He does not attempt to oppose stresses and allows them to encroach, and then absorbs them without apparent response.

The passive or compliant person seems easy to help because he takes advice readily, but he may be too lacking in drive to follow advice about positive action. The danger is that he becomes over-dependent on others, so that anyone trying to help him becomes too dominant and starts to live his life for him.

The *aggressive* individual is basically truculent and hostile, with a chip on his shoulder. He is opposed for opposition's sake and not necessarily because something or someone is wrong. He has little concern for the feelings of others and tramples people underfoot. He generates his own stresses in his dealings both with things and with people. Aggressive people often respond badly to stress which tends to make them more hostile, often in an undirected way.

The aggressive person seeks advice in a positive way but usually does not act on it, unless it confirms his own ideas.

Only if things go very wrong and the aggressive person becomes chastened, does he become amenable to discussion and advice.

The word *neurotic* as a personality trait is usually applied to people who show excessive behaviour characteristics and exaggerated or over-emotional responses. Almost by definition, neurotic implies abnormally high susceptibility and reaction to stress. The unpredictability of behaviour is such that it can be difficult to identify the source of stress, especially as the person puts out misleading clues. What appears to be the source of stress may be innocuous and what appears neutral or even supportive may be stressful to the person.

ways of coping

First, the cause of stress should be identified and scrutinised; sometimes a change in attitudes could resolve the problem. Adapting to stress can bring about changes which are often all to the good. Other stresses, particularly not of our making, could be eased by taking definite steps such as changing jobs, or moving house, or even, if it has to be, getting divorced.

In some cases, the only solution is to come to terms with unpleasant realities since they are there to stay. Accepting them once and for all lessens their stressful impact.

It is important at all times to keep a positive self-image and not to indulge in self-fulfilling negative prophecies. Whenever you attempt a new way of coping with stress, whether you succeed or not, do a kind of de-briefing afterwards. Ask yourself what went well and what went wrong, how you might have handled things differently; think about it and tell yourself all the positive and useful aspects of what you did. You can learn from any experience, good or bad.

It is important but often difficult to recognise the true and relevant sources of stress; much effort can be needlessly expended in trying to neutralise or remove wrongly-assumed sources of stress.

Stress in one circumstance may spill over and influence another situation. For example, a man stressed at work may come home in an irritable, explosive state, so that domestic friction arises. Domestic friction may lead to preoccupation and inattention at work, and poor work performance, putting the job in jeopardy which increases the marital problem. The factors interact and stress builds up from both. Trying to tackle them means first sorting out which of them is the original cause and how they interact. Unconscious defence mechanisms of the mind, such as rationalisation or projection, may need to be brought to light first.

denying and distorting

Some ways of dealing with stress derive from the inability to face unpleasant reality and may contain a degree of denying or distorting reality. These mechanisms are similar to some every-day mental processes, in an extreme form; the difference is one of degree rather than of kind.

Rationalisation is a means of self-deception by which a person finds satisfactory and socially acceptable reasons for conduct. Rationalisation comes into play in a 'sour grapes' situation when someone who fails in his objective then claims that the prize was not worth having. A man who fails to gain promotion may minimise stress by asserting that the pro-motion would have had so many disadvantages that he is better off as he is. Sometimes the spouse will collude with this rationalisation, in which case harmony is maintained. If the spouse refuses to enter into the deception, this may create another source of stress.

Projection is the attribution of personal shortcomings and failures to the environment and other people, as exemplified by the bad workman blaming his tools, or the incompetent executive blaming everyone but himself for his failures. In a more extreme form, projection can become paranoia, the per-son becoming deluded in his blame of others.

Displacement is the diverting of emotional emphasis from one object or person to another. Displacement activities include the enthusiastic espousal of a hobby when promotion is blocked at work or when there is marital friction.

Displacement activity can take the form of biologically inappropriate activity when an appropriate one is blocked, such as banging one's fist on the table instead of into the rival's face, kicking the cat instead of one's spouse.

Withdrawal is more passive – the stressed person throws in the sponge and attempts to retire emotionally from the situation by daydreaming and becoming apathetic. The stress no longer elicits any response – nor does anything else, however.

Partial withdrawal is seen in nostalgia, where the stressed person reverts to the past, usually forgetting the unpleasant things and dwelling on his past successes. Many old people succumb to this, as their way of coping with the stress of having no future.

Regression is a more complete reversion, not just to the past but to an earlier childhood state. Under stress, even robust personalities may yearn to return to a state of dependency in which they were protected and decisions made for them. Sometimes this regressive tendency is actively encouraged as, for example, in hospitals where nursing and medical staff, conniving with relatives, render the patient passive and dependent.

Denial means quite simply persuading oneself that something is not so, in the hope that it will not be so. If we tell ourselves that problems do not exist, perhaps they will go away. If we shut our eyes so that we cannot see something, perhaps it is not there.

One way of trying to deal with stress is to deny that anything is amiss or needs facing up to. The person denies the existence of problems and difficulties whenever they are raised by others, and most of all he denies them to himself, in an attempt to safeguard his emotional security or self-esteem. He may succeed in dodging the stress for the time being. But relationships with others are likely to suffer and may be irretrievably

damaged through the person's persistent refusal to acknowledge that problems exist. Friends, relatives, colleagues and
anyone else involved with the person are often left feeling
frustrated or angry. They can help by making it as easy as
possible for the denier to change his stance without losing face
– not saying 'at last you are seeing sense, you fool' but 'I think
you may have a point there' as a starting point for tackling the
hitherto-denied problem.

previous coping

A useful mental exercise for the stressed person is to remember
how he dealt with similar problems in the past. If he coped in
the past, he should ask himself "Why am I not coping now?"
The answer may help him to identify the problem. The stress
may be greater, more persistent or mean more to him. For
example, threat of redundancy is much more stressful to a man
when he has a family to support than when he is a footloose
bachelor. The stressed person may find it more difficult to cope
because of several untoward happenings in quick succession,
or physical ill health, or greater age.

Previous coping may have involved behaviour which the
stressed person can no longer use. For example, he may have
blamed others for his deficiencies in his job but finds that this
excuse no longer works. Sometimes, stress has been borne
with the help of a particular person, relative or friend, who is
no longer available: without their support, the person cannot
cope alone.

self-perception

As far as stress is concerned, how people see themselves is
more important than the reality of their situation and is a major
factor in coping or not coping. Stress responses are largely
determined by, for instance, the perceived threat to emotional
security or to self-esteem. Changing the perception of the

stress – how one views it – can mitigate the effect of the stress or neutralise it completely.

attitudes and delusions

The 20th century myth that 'happiness' should be actively striven for sets up unreal expectations. One activity which may well be modified is trying too hard to pursue happiness. Much unhappiness, discontent and sense of futility can be avoided by modifying one's attitude towards the more sensible goal of avoiding or removing known sources of unhappiness, rather than consciously trying to pursue happiness.

Another delusive hope is the belief that 'once such-and-such is out of the way, I shall be happy', because undoubtedly another obstacle will occur to postpone this state of utopia. It is better to try and analyse the reasons for the present discontent. Then you can decide whether you can do something to alter it, or have to make the best of a bad job.

Rather than blaming the past for our present difficulties and inadequacies, it should be examined for lessons it can give us about dealing with problems in the future. Nor should one dwell too lovingly on the past. Comparing the present with 'the good old days' is a recipe for discontent and stress, because the mind forgets the bad things and views the good through nostalgic rose-tinted spectacles.

aspirations, ambitions, recognition

Many people set their expectations too high so that when, inevitably, some goals are missed and there are no outstanding achievements, a sense of failure and futility sets in and ordinary problems become magnified to stresses.

People's aspirations vary enormously from the brash individual who wants to conquer the world to the diffident, self-effacing type who truly believes that the meek will inherit the earth. When ambition drives a person on, to beyond his capabilities, stress will mount as the realisation dawns that the goals are unattainable. Even worse than unattained ambition is slipping back, demotion, with loss of status and therefore loss of self-esteem. A sense of failure and worthlessness may then follow.

Resetting goals realistically and re-assessing achievements as worthwhile, even if modest, should lessen the sense of inadequacy. A realistic view of your own strengths and shortcomings is an important step in reducing stress. It is difficult to be rational and honest about one's own short-comings, so be prepared to listen to, and not reject without thinking, other people's assessment of your capabilities.

When you are satisfied with your own performance, you should not need to be told by others how good you are in order to enjoy and appreciate what you have achieved. Where praise does come from outsiders, savour it, as an actor would applause.

Knowing what a pleasant thing praise is, if you, in your turn, admire something that someone else has done or achieved, say so – being told may be the one bright moment in that person's day.

detachment

If you can cultivate an ability to stand back, and view your activities in as detached a way as possible, you may be able to learn to distinguish between difficulties of your own making or capable of being lessened, and those which are immutable. When you realise what is truly beyond your control, you can stop trying to alter it. Some people only begin to cope with stress when they finally accept that much of life is full of uncertainties.

Activities and emotions which seem terribly important to the person involved at the time, may seem ridiculous viewed from another angle. Petty rivalries at work or bickering in the family which might build up into stressful situations can be defused by a sense of the ridiculous and the absurd.

helping others

Matters that are outside personal control and are yet a source of concern and worry are a source of stress. Many people have general fears for mankind in the nuclear age. Those who actively campaign for sanity and survival and join activist groups, for instance to protect the environment, may or may not achieve the major goal, but may feel less stressed by going out and trying to do something about it (plus the solidarity of likeminded spirits) than those who just sit and worry.

There may be community activities and projects to get involved in, if only, for example, helping to clear and reclaim waste land for a children's playground. Initiating such a project, or opposing bureaucratic schemes, or agitating for a by-pass road to prevent a village being pounded by heavy lorries, enables some people to find a purpose in life. But such displacement activities should not be allowed to take over as a new source of stress.

Helping others can be a worthwhile (and stress-reducing) activity. But even voluntary work should be disciplined and done on a regular basis. Visiting an old lady or two when the whim occurs may help neither the visitor nor the visited.

Group activities are usually more stress-reducing than solitary ones because of the social aspect of meeting new people.

social contacts

Increasing social contacts can lessen stress by widening one's interests. Getting out of social isolation may need effort and one must be prepared to give more than one receives – which is not always easy when going through a rough patch oneself, but worth trying.

Some people overvalue outside relationships and priorities, such as work and career, and undervalue the real most personal relationships: those of husband/wife, child/parent, close friends – people for whom one can do something directly and personally. You cannot change the whole world and make it a better place, but you can help to make your family and immediate circle of friends a happier one. Finding something or somebody to care about helps to give a sense of purpose. But be careful not to invest new friends, new goals and new sources of interest with a magical or overrated significance.

Support from the family is a most important protection against the effects of stress. It is therefore particularly important that conflicts within the family should be resolved, if this mutual support is to be achieved.

pets

Because the relationship with a pet is relatively stable and uncomplicated, keeping a pet has been advocated as helpful for mentally distressed people when convalescing after an acute breakdown. Many people remark how relaxing a pet can be. Certainly, a disdainful cat who refuses to be hustled into doing anything against its wishes and the unquestioning loyalty and affection of a dog can each illustrate some fundamental values in life.

A dog has the added advantage of needing to be taken for walks, played with, and taken care of to a greater extent than that independent creature, the cat. Even a cat curling up on one's lap asking to be stroked, or sitting by the fireside and making the room feel lived-in, can help people to relax during periods of stress.

But do not expect too much from your pet or treat it as if it were a child. And if the pet does not meet your needs, do not lose interest in it and leave it to fend for itself.

religious activities

To some people, the most supportive of group activities is active participation in religious practices, the common theme of a system of beliefs held by a group of people. This can range from occasional acts of worship and prayer to complex codes of conduct which govern the relationship between man and man, man and his environment, man and his creator.

The support given by religion is compounded of the existence of a corpus of shared beliefs which transcends rationality and can lend meaning and a structure to life, plus the feeling of belonging to a group of like-minded people.

Pressures to conform may, however, be extreme in some of the more highly organised religious denominations and sects; if the person conflicts with the group beliefs, or challenges the authority of the established religious figures, he may be excluded from the group. This loss of support and alienation can be very stressful. But, in general, if the spirit of the religious beliefs is adhered to, stress can be markedly alleviated.

As well as spiritual support, many religious organisations provide practical help, and many charities are linked to religious bodies. Some churches organise relief for the needy of the locality and are open much of the day on an emergency basis.

Many people, who are otherwise irregular in their observance, turn to religion at times of bereavement and personal crisis. The ritualisation of the burial ceremony can help people to come to terms with loss. Many ministers of religion, even if unworldy and unable to help with many practical matters, are experienced in counselling the stressed and will not refuse help if it can reasonably be given.

retreats

It is not necessary to be a believer, or to be committed to any religion, to go on a retreat although many people go in the spirit of seeking God.

A retreat is an opportunity to withdraw from the rush of life in order to be still, listen and discern the deeper realities of life. It is a period of anything from a few days to a month or more which is consciously set apart for rest and some sort of spiritual input. The experience is different for each individual. Some people go on a private retreat, they make their own plan for spending their time within a convent, monastery or retreat house setting.

Retreats are not necessarily silent although the importance of silence is recognised. In most retreats, provision is made for people who need to talk to someone about their life or problems.

Ø **National Retreat Centre**, Liddon House, 24 South Audley Street, London W1Y 5DL (telephone 01-493 3534) is an ecumenical association and includes the Association for Promoting Retreats, the National Retreat Movement (Roman Catholic) and the Methodist Retreat Group. It provides an information service and publishes the journal *The Vision* (80p) which includes a list of houses offering accommodation (in alphabetical order of county) to individual retreatants or groups, with a calendar of retreat events which include drop-in days, yoga workshops, silent retreats, religious and lay retreats.

LEARNING TO RELAX

Stress-reducing procedures which can be learned include relaxation, meditation, self-hypnosis and autosuggestion, biofeedback, coping in imagination. They have many elements in common, and people vary as to which they find helpful. If one type of approach is unsuccessful or helps only a little, another may be more acceptable and useful.

Some techniques are more advanced than others. For instance, it is impossible to meditate if you are unable to relax. Learning to relax takes time and practice. But do not let that deter you: you do not need to become highly proficient in order to derive some benefit.

progressive relaxation

An increase in muscle tension is often the first sign of mounting stress. Muscle tension and mental tension go hand in hand, the state of mind and the state of body each reinforcing the other. Learning to relax the body can help relax the mind.

The overall principle of progressive relaxation is that each of the main muscle groups in the body is first tensed, then held taut, and then relaxed in turn, until the whole body is relaxed. The idea is that before you can relax your body, you must learn how your muscles feel when they are tight and tense. Letting go after tensing gives a physically pleasant feeling in the relaxed muscles. It is essential to develop this awareness of the difference between muscle tension and muscle relaxation. Try clenching the hand into a fist, holding it tight for a little while and then letting go, appreciating the feeling of release. Or hunch up your shoulders, stay that way, and then let all the muscles go.

Relaxation methods involving tensing the muscles are not

recommended by some doctors for people with hypertension (high blood pressure).

The best way to learn relaxation is probably by attending a class, with a live teacher. It is also possible to buy tapes or records giving instructions for you to follow, or you may be able to get hold of some written instructions which a friend or relative could read out to you. Alternatively, you could your-self record the instructions on to a tape and play it back when you want it.

how to do it

If you want to practise relaxation, you should allow at least a quarter of an hour a day and try to follow the same sequence every time.

Relaxing surroundings are helpful but not essential. It is best (at least at first) to choose a quiet, dimly-lit room where you can be warm and comfortable and not subject to distractions. Relaxation should be enjoyable, otherwise it will not work. Begin by taking off your shoes and loosening any tight cloth-ing, especially at the neck and waist. Adopt a relaxing posture: the easiest is probably lying down.

Lie down on a carpeted floor, or a bed – provided it is not too soft. All parts of your body should be supported comfortably. Lie with your arms and legs a little apart. It is better to do without a pillow.

> You should tense and relax each part of your body in turn, starting either with hands and arms, then head and down through the trunk to the legs, or starting with the feet and legs and working up through the body.
>
> If you begin with the hands and arms, you should first clench the fists, which also entails clenching the forearm muscles. Hold this for a little while, perhaps 10 seconds, and feel the tension; then let go and feel the difference – a sensation of welcome release. Then hold the hands (fists clenched) against the shoulders so as to tense the upper arms, feel the tension, and then let go.

Next the neck can be held taut with the chin pressed in, then relaxed, followed by the different facial muscles – forehead (frown and relax), eyebrows (raise up then release), eyes, mouth (purse up and release), jaw (thrust forward and release), then the shoulders (hunch up then let go), stomach, buttocks, thighs, legs and feet. Each time you should consciously feel the tension before you let go.

After tensing and relaxing each muscle group in turn, you should feel relaxed all over. Instead of thinking of yourself in parts, be aware of the whole body and if you feel any remaining tension anywhere, try to release it – if necessary by first deliberately tensing the affected muscles and then letting go.

Allow 5 to 10 minutes at the end in which to enjoy your relaxed state. You should be breathing quietly, with slow and gentle breaths. You may want to imagine a peaceful scene, for instance lying peacefully by the side of a blue lake, with green grass and trees, the song of the birds, the warmth of the sun, your body warm, heavy and relaxed. Choose your own imagined scene – whatever you like best.

When you are ready to get up, first have a good stretch, then either sit up very slowly or turn over (onto your side first into what is called 'the recovery position') then get up.

Your aim should be to carry over your relaxed state into whatever activity follows your period of relaxation.

Although it is easier to practise relaxation while lying down, sitting is also all right. You can practise in an armchair – and in time you should be able to relax even in an office chair or on a bus or in the driver's seat of a parked car, or wherever you happen to be.

staying relaxed

Once the technique of relaxation has been learned, it should be possible to relax without first tensing all the muscles and it should be easy to detect any areas of tenseness and quickly release the tension in these areas.

Throughout the day, get into the habit of checking whether you are tensing any muscles unnecessarily. If you are, you are not only wasting energy and effort but could well bring on headache, neckache, and backache.

If your face is tensed and mouth turned downward, relax it and consciously force the corners of your lips upwards into a smile. It may be mechanical, but helps you to feel less dejected or stressed.

Ø **Relaxation for living**, 29 Burwood Park Road, Walton on Thames, Surrey KT12 5LH promotes the teaching of relaxation techniques to combat stress, anxiety and tension. There is a countrywide network of teachers. The classes may include some teaching about physiology, psychology and nutrition. A correspondence course is available for people unable to attend classes. Apart from the list of qualified teachers who run relaxation classes throughout England, there are tapes and literature.

Ø **Lifeskills**, 3 Brighton Road, London N2 8JU (telephone 01-346 9646) is an organisation which provides books and tape cassette programmes by mail order which can help people handle stressful experiences, such as flying or exams. They also organise seminars.

meditation

Relaxation does not just mean reducing muscle tension. It is equally important, if not more so, to achieve a peaceful state of mind. Meditation is a way of learning control of the mind, with the object of increasing quietness of mind. When the mind is still, it may become possible to see through problems. In the course of meditation, the meditator comes to understand the transient nature of all things, that feelings such as anger, hate and love come and go and are not with one for ever. When a person understands that nothing is permanent, he may become calm and serene; suffering diminishes when it is realised that nothing belongs to anyone. Such thinking is part of Buddhist philosophy.

Meditation is a feature of many disciplines and religions. But it can, of course, be undertaken by anyone of any religion, or of none.

Many schools of meditation have developed, or been adopted in the west, and some extravagant claims have been made. But simple meditation techniques have been shown to reduce stress responses in many people.

During meditation (and probably during other stress-reducing techniques) oxygen consumption and depth of breathing decrease, heart rate slows down and the brain waves assume the pattern characteristic of relaxation, while mental alertness is unimpaired. In some Buddhist teaching, meditation is taught through systematic techniques. First of all it is necessary to control the mind, to know what is being thought. This can be achieved through focusing the mind on the rising and falling of the breath. Meditation may then take the form of fixing the thought on one single object which can be external or a thought within. The nub of the procedure is to focus attention very narrowly, either on a specific object such as a flower, or on a special word (a 'mantra') which is repeated in imagination. The person sits quietly engaged in this simple activity: he is essentially doing nothing, in itself a relief from the pressure of everyday life. He must let his attention be focused without that becoming an active process. Meditating is attending to that focus in a mindful, aware way. If attention lapses, it is easy to fall asleep.

When a distracting thought drifts into consciousness, the mind should be gently led back to the chosen word, sound, or visual symbol.

where to do it

The environment should be relaxing – a quiet room, dimmed lights, no telephone to ring unexpectedly. The meditator sits (or lies) in a comfortable position; clothing should be comfortable and unrestricting. Meditating for about 10–15 minutes twice a day is what should be aimed at, but once a person knows how to do it, even a couple of minutes' meditation at any time can help to counteract the build-up of stress. If meditating regularly, it is beneficial to be 'checked' by an experienced practitioner from time to time, to ensure that you are using the right sort of method for you, and using it correctly.

Meditation classes are available at many adult education centres. Some experienced practitioners are happy to give private or group lessons but it is important that they do not abuse the trust of their pupils by making extravagant claims – or charging extravagant fees.

Although the technique is easy to learn, meditation may not have immediate appeal. The whole process may at first seem too passive. It involves doing virtually nothing and this does not come naturally to people in our culture.

autogenic training

Autogenics was developed as a deep relaxation technique more than fifty years ago, based on the principles of eastern meditation (but not related to any religion). It is a technique for obtaining voluntary control over the involuntary nervous system which would modify an individual's reaction to stress. The relaxed state achieved by autogenic training has been described as a state of passive concentration.

Autogenics is taught as a series of easy mental exercises designed to switch off the stress system and switch on the relaxation system. Once you have learned the technique, it can become part of your lifestyle. Courses usually consist of eight one-hour sessions, either individually or in a group.

how it is done

In autogenic training, you lie or sit in a quiet place and are taught to repeat phrases which suggest that particular parts of the body are getting heavy and warm and that the mind is at rest. This should induce deep relaxation and reduce stress and make a person respond more readily to positive auto-suggestions.

Conditions which have been known to respond to autogenic training include some stress-related disorders. However, people who have suffered from heart trouble, stroke, high or low blood pressure, epilepsy, diabetes or been under psychiatric treatment, should not try the method without first consulting their doctor.

As in meditation, autogenics brings about the opposite physical symptoms to stress: a lowering of the metabolic rate, a decrease in heart and respiration rates and a change in brainwaves pattern – all physiological signs of deep relaxation.

Sometimes people who are learning the method may find that when they are in a state of deep relaxation they recall distressing episodes from their past. Reliving these old traumas can be a useful experience because it allows the person to release pent-up feeling which may have been contributing to his stress. But people are strongly advised to train under the supervision of a doctor or psychotherapist (individually or in a group), so that the recall of distressing experience can then be handled with the help of the therapist. Autogenics is not a self-help technique and should not be embarked upon on one's own. Attempts to 'learn' autogenic training therapy from commercial tapes are likely to achieve little, or even produce worrying experiences.

Ø **Centre for autogenic training**, Positive Health Centre, 101 Harley Street, London W1N 1DF (telephone 01-935 1811) will, on request, send a list of qualified doctors and health professionals trained and recommended by the centre, with a warning against therapists who have no professional training which qualifies them to use this specific technique.

hypnotherapy and self-hypnosis

In the hypnotic state, control of the mind is not given up to the hypnotist. Nor is hypnosis a form of sleep: it is a state of altered awareness, in which the person focuses on a set of suggestions and allows himself to be receptive to them.

In the hypnotic state, people accept suggestions that lessen their tension and anxiety and they can be instructed gradually to improve disturbed behaviour.

In the hypnotic treatment of anxieties, continuous suggestions of relaxation are given by the therapist. The person is asked to imagine stress-producing situations and sees that he can remain calm and controlled while visualising various stresses. Subsequently, should any such situation arise in the course of his daily life, the person will have learned to deal with it, without stressful reactions reappearing.

Nowadays, hypnotherapy is taught in some medical schools and is used by some doctors, dentists and clinical and research psychologists. There are also lay hypnotists who may be without medical knowledge. It is not excessively difficult to hypnotise someone, but only a trained person knows what to do next.

self-hypnosis

Doctors who use hypnosis teach their patients self-hypnosis so that at a time of stress they can immediately produce in themselves a relaxed and altered state, free from anxiety.

To succeed with self-hypnosis needs an open mind, genuine motivation, time, a quiet place and an effective set of hypnotic suggestions. The aim is to feel relaxed, and receptive to suggestions from within or from without.

People can learn to hypnotise themselves without an outsider. But it is easier, and generally better, to start with a medical teacher.

how it is done

The most widely used method for inducing a hypnotic state is to fix your attention on an object, preferably one requiring the eyes to turn upwards and so inducing a certain degree of fatigue. As you look at it, you should tell yourself that your eyelids will get heavier and heavier until they close and that at that point you have reached a state of relaxation and full awareness. Repeat this suggestion at intervals of about a minute. Concentrate on the heaviness of your eyelids until they close. Become aware of your breathing. Take a deep breath, hold it, then breathe out slowly, saying to yourself 'relax'. Beware of trying too hard. Let your breathing be slow and regular. Deal with any residual tension you may be feeling by saying to yourself that you will relax more deeply every time you breathe out.

The second phase, concerned with deepening the hypnotic state, is achieved by slow, deep, breathing and the help of any visual imagery that can suggest a sense of downward or upward movement.

You can then proceed to suggestions concerning your behaviour, thought and feelings, formulating resolves to change in various ways. In later sessions, you will be reiterating these as necessary, by way of reinforcement, and you may be formulating new ones. Suggestions are more effective if they are repeated and phrased positively ("I shall . . .", rather than "I shall not . . .", avoid also "I'll try . . .", which suggests that you might fail). What you are doing is to foster in yourself a feeling of control over yourself and your environment. Visual fantasy images in which you picture yourself doing what you say you are going to do are often even more effective than verbal suggestions.

You can come out of even a deep hypnotic state at will with a countdown, in which you tell yourself that you will surface after counting to five.

coping in imagination

Rehearsing how to deal with a particular situation, something that we have all done at some time, can be deliberately practised as a stress-reducing manoeuvre. It involves confronting, in imagination, a stressful situation (several times if necessary) without becoming panicky or retreating from the scene.

As with other relaxation techniques, start by becoming relaxed and comfortable in quiet surroundings. Next, while relaxed, envisage and focus on the stressful situation.

The feelings of anxiety or anger or disgust that develop should be held in check by breathing slowly and deeply, or actively relaxing some groups of muscles, as in progressive relaxation. Tell yourself not to worry but to work out how to cope with the situation; rehearse in your mind various ways of dealing with it. Do not select just one method of coping but think through several alternatives, and get clear in the mind where your resistance lies and how much compromise is possible. Envisage the worst consequences of the situation and then assess whether it is really as bad as you had thought. Remember how you coped before, and try to do the same again – or analyse why it is not possible this time, and what you can do instead.

Then switch off and try to forget about it all, by concentrating on a relaxing image, such as a fine view seen on holiday. After a few minutes, the whole sequence can be repeated.

role-playing

A useful variation of this method, which needs the help of someone else, is role-playing in which you act your own part and the helper that of the antagonist. Role-playing is a good way of rehearsing how you will deal with a situation. A difficult or feared situation (such as how to say 'no') is realistically rehearsed until the stress goes out of it and, hopefully, will not come back when the scene is re-enacted in reality.

Role-playing where you act both parts (and speak them

aloud and swap chairs with yourself) can help to give you an insight into the conflict that may be causing the stress.

biofeedback

This method was introduced in the late '60s, as a means of facilitating relaxation and reducing anxiety, and helping the treatment of some stress-related conditions. It was hailed as a miracle treatment for a number of conditions. The early claims made on behalf of the therapeutic value of the technique have yet to be confirmed. But biofeedback is useful to show people 'scientifically' that they are tense, especially when they do not feel stressed or are unaware of it themselves.

It is essentially a technique which tries to make the individual aware of changes in bodily responses and functions as they happen, with the aim that he should gradually be able to control those functions.

Biofeedback involves the use of devices which provide constant (visual or aural) information about the state of tension or relaxation. Heart rate can be monitored and recorded, so can muscle activity and sweating on the palms of the hands. The pattern of brainwaves can be recorded. The biofeedback machine measures physical response to stress and flashes a signal to the person using it when his anxiety level starts to rise. Over a period of time, the person can learn to lower the signal by consciously relaxing, until eventually he is able to control feelings of anxiety or stress without needing to use the machine.

how it is done
The person tries to change the reading of the machine so that the indicator will move in the right direction, or the noise stop, or whatever is the machine's indication of 'greater relaxation' – and by doing so, may be able to achieve greater relaxation.

Biofeedback machines in use in hospital departments are fairly complex and are used in connection with research. Small and relatively inexpensive devices are available to the public, for use at home or anywhere else. Those for monitoring muscular tension or sweating are the simplest to operate; the sweat-measuring ones are the least expensive. There are pocket-sized instruments that look like a small transistor radio, and cost around £60 each. A person's degree of sweating, reflecting his level of tension or relaxation, is picked up by two small electrodes, attached to fingertips or the palm, and feedback information is given as a continuous tone or click, through an earphone no bigger than a hearing aid. Some people derive encouragement from seeing the success of their attempts recorded by a machine.

EXERCISE AND RECREATION

Exercise and sport are excellent ways of lessening stress and of preventing some of its damaging effects on the body. Also, sleep at night tends to be sounder following exercise during the day. Exercise can be taken irregularly, perhaps when stresses begin to mount up, or, better, as a regular routine. It can range from a long walk in the country to a brisk game of football or squash.

If the person is inherently competitive, instead of alleviating stress, leisure activities may add to it. Some joggers doggedly insist on their 5 miles a day, come what may, and become stressed if they fail to attain their goal. Worries over golf handicaps or how well the team is doing can become exaggerated.

Sport and exercise must be a relaxation if they are to serve as safety valves against stress, and should not be invested with a special significance, lest they, in turn, become a stress.

The report "Why Exercise?" in the December 1987 issue of *Self-Health* summarises what and how long-lasting are the beneficial effects of exercise.

yoga

In this country, many people practice hatha yoga which consists of postures, movements and breathing exercises and specific relaxation processes. They do this mainly because it is a discipline which gives them a sense of well-being, makes them feel relaxed, and physically fit.

Yoga has been developed as a way of life that people practise in order to find new avenues of spiritual development. The posture and the breathing techniques are designed to exercise the whole body systematically, to improve the circulation of the blood throughout the body. The physical changes associated with all forms of yoga help to reduce stress. The aim of the discipline is that the mind, too, should become free from everyday tension.

Although yoga can be learned, to some extent, from books, it is better to attend a class, at least to begin with, if only to be shown the right postures – and for the encouragement of practising in the company of others.

Ø **The Yoga for Health Foundation**, Ickwell Bury, Biggleswade, Bedfordshire SG18 9EF (telephone 076-727 271) maintains a residential centre and runs local groups in Britain and many other countries.

Most local authorities offer yoga and relaxation classes as part of their adult education programme. Local newspapers and yoga journals and leisure-activity magazines carry details of classes, both subsidised and private.

Ø **The British Wheel of Yoga**, 1 Hamilton Place, Boston Road, Sleaford, Lincolnshire NG34 7ES (telephone 0529-306851) aims to encourage and help people to a greater knowledge and understanding of all aspects of yoga and its practice by the provision of education and training; to maintain and improve the standard of teaching and to co-operate with and support other organisations having similar aims. There are nearly one thousand teachers holding The Wheel's diploma, and over 100 teacher education tutors.

Many local education authorities will only accept holders of the Wheel Diploma to teach yoga in further education classes.

The British Wheel of Yoga is a member of the Central Council for Physical Recreation. The Wheel co-operates with other yoga organisations in Great Britain and internationally.

T'ai-Chi Ch'uan

The present form of T'ai-chi dates from 14th century China. Even then it was recognised that anxiety, irritation and fear, by causing tension can cause disease through interfering with breathing, circulation and general functioning of the body.

T'ai-chi Ch'uan is a discipline of mind and body based on the belief that man was created to function as an integrated whole. It uses body movement (callisthenics) to promote health of mind and body.

In physical terms, it helps to relax the whole body and to deepen breathing, to improve co-ordination, to loosen joints, increase flexibility, and – in more subtle terms – it teaches self-control, develops patience and perseverance. The movements are rhythmic cycles with a constant fluid shifting of body weight, with spiral movements of the arms. To the onlooker it appears as a gentle, contemplative slow-moving dance. Unlike yoga, there is no holding of postures and no stretching.

T'ai-chi cannot be easily learnt from a book: it requires personal practical guidance, especially in body alignment and relaxation. It is best learned by attending in a group or a class of at least 1½ hours a week (benefits should begin from the first lesson).

Since terms and instructions vary, it would be wise to make personal contact with the instructor and watch a class, if possible, before enrolling.

Classes are held at adult education centres and other places, and once you have learned the movements and philosophy behind them, you will be able to carry on by yourself.

Ø **School of T'ai-Chi Ch'uan**, 5 Tavistock Place, London WC1 (telephone 01-459 0764) offers introductory courses and further information.

some strategies

○ Be aware of possible stressors, in what context they are likely
  to make their impact on your health, and which factors
  increase your vulnerability – then take steps to avoid
  unnecessary factors.
○ Try to develop a flexible attitude, accepting other people's
  intolerance.
○ Reduce unrealistically high expectations of your own performance, to increase your sense of accomplishment.
○ Learn to express emotions by developing assertiveness, by
  learning to speak up for your rights politely but firmly and
  communicating your needs clearly while at the same time
  respecting other people's needs.
○ Ask for help from others, your spouse, lover, friends and
  family, community leaders, members of church or other
  religious, social, political or recreational organisations;
  health care providers can offer support in case of need in a
  variety of ways and thus reduce the impact of stress.
○ Take actions to increase your resistance by proper nutrition,
  adequate exercise, developing a healthy life-style and avoiding smoking, excessive alcohol and a fatty diet.

improving your health

Improving your health in general can help lessen the effects of
stress on the body. Everyone knows how minor infections
multiply when you are feeling run down, and how chronic
aches and pains become magnified.

Some commonsense measures to improve general health
include not smoking, eating a sensible diet, getting proper
sleep, taking regular exercise, including specific relaxation
exercises, and cutting down on excessive alcohol. While, in
strict moderation, alcohol may do more good than harm in
alleviating mild stress, moderation is the key word. Taking

alcohol solely to alleviate major or prolonged stress is a way of dealing with only the symptom and not with the cause. Moreover, there is the threat of becoming dependent on alcohol if it is used as a way of tackling problems.

hobbies

Regular leisure activities are important in reducing stress. People should make time for positive leisure pursuits rather than, say, spending 2–3 hours each evening watching television (although that, too, can be relaxing).

The spare-time gardener whose vegetables may not win prizes but which can be eaten, the amateur photographer whose prints may not be displayed in the local library but are admired by the family, the cyclist who does not do untold miles a day but discovers out-of-the-way villages, get much satisfaction form their activities. The satisfaction often comes from the doing rather than from the results. Someone taking up painting, for example, will not be discouraged if a still-life turns out looking like an abstract. The idea lies in the activity.

Groups of enthusiasts usually welcome someone new who wishes to take up 'their' hobby and may offer the use of equipment so that the newcomer can make sure he really has an interest before laying out money on it.

Adult education institutes run day and evening classes and the list of subjects available in the larger centres is often staggering in its length and variety. Local hobby groups often display advertisements in the local library, civic centre or the local newspaper.

laughter and singing

In Sweden, an experiment is being carried out by a small group to relieve stress through laughter. The men and women, all suffering from industrial ailments, meet once a week and recall amusing things that may have happened to them and look at funny material, amusing books, films and jokes. The theory is that when one laughs, the muscles relax and stress is diminished.

In England, the value of laughter is recognised by the Stress Foundation which recommends:

○ listening to funny radio programmes and watching funny videos
○ drawing a smiling face on a piece of card and looking at it when depression hits
○ introducing humour to counteract stress at work
○ lifting your spirits by listening to music.

Singing, as anyone who does it regularly knows, is an unparalleled unraveller of tension. This can be partly explained by the need for correct breathing to produce the right sound but it is also a primitive and uninhibited form of self-expression.

INDEX

INDEX

abdominal
– breathing, 24
– pain, 18
abnormal depression, 119–126
absentmindedness, 36
Accept, 38
accidents, 68, 80, 88, 89, 103
Action on Smoking and Health, 36
activities, 79, 151, 159
acupuncture, 131, 132
adapting, 14, 47, 50, 58, 65, 74, 75
addiction, 38, 123, 124
adolescence, 59, 60, 103
adoption, 51
adrenaline, 13, 14, 19, 33, 93, 100,
    102, 104
adrenocortical hormone, 13
adrenomedullary hormones, 13
aggression, 37, 51, 55, 72, 79, 105,
    142, 144
agitated depression, 19
agoraphobia, 118
AIDS, 60
air traffic controller, 87
air travel, 82
aircraft, 76, 82
airline pilot, 87
Al-Anon Family Groups UK & Eire,
    38
Alateen, 38
alcohol, 17, 82, 107, 111, 122, 139,
    170, 171
– abstinence, 38
– dependence, 37, 38
Alcohol Concern, 38
Alcoholics Anonymous, 38
Alexander technique, 26
All Wales Drugsline, 124
allergy, 99, 101
alopecia areata, 102
alternative medicine, 131 et seq.
Alzheimer's Disease Society, 44

ambition, 149
analgesics, 25, 111
anger, 19, 33, 43, 45, 51, 60, 61, 66,
    69, 72, 96, 105, 112, 139, 158, 164
angina pectoris, 17, 100
anguish, 44, 69
animals, 76, 77
anorexia nervosa, 32
antacid, 110, 112
anti-depressant, 121, 129, 131
anticipatory anxiety, 71, 84
antihistamine, 99, 122
anxiety, 16, 17, 19, 20, 22, 23, 32, 33,
    36, 37, 43, 47, 50, 53, 58, 59, 60,
    65, 67, 78, 80, 81, 91, 93, 96, 100,
    101, 112, 113, 116–128, 129, 130,
    132, 139, 142, 143, 158, 162, 164,
    165
apathy, 61, 147
appetite, 18, 121, 122
appetite suppressants, 122
apprehension, 64
argument, 24, 40, 51, 52
Arthritis and Rheumatism Council,
    114
aspirin, 111
assault, 55, 83
assertion, 37, 52, 60, 71, 72, 73, 170
Association of Carers, 73
Asthma Society and Friends of the
    Asthma Research Council, 101
atheroma, 100, 104
attachment, 65, 66
attention, 34, 159
attitudes, 9, 10, 53, 94, 142, 149, 170
autogenic exercises, 93
autogenic training, 160, 161
autonomy, lack of at work, 89
autosuggestion, 155, 161, 163
awareness, 162, 163

baby, 50, 57, 63, 68, 120

baby-battering, 55
baby-blues, 170
backache, 16, 112, 120, 158
– support, 79
Balance, 104
baldness, 102
behaviour changes, 10, 16, 44, 60, 67
benzodiazepines, 122
bereavement, 16, 44, 46, 64, 65, 118, 119, 137, 153
– counselling, 46
beta-blocker, 100
biofeedback, 131, 155, 165, 166
birth, 9
– of sibling, 50, 57
bladder, 13, 18, 22
blood
– flow, 14, 19, 26, 80, 100, 167
– pressure, 12, 14, 17, 78, 106, 107, 122, 131, 155, 161
– vessels, 12, 17, 78, 100, 104, 106, 109
blue-collar workers, 87
bodily response, 14, 15 *et seq.*
bodily symptoms, 10, 136
body clock, 21, 87, 88
boredom, 33, 36, 87, 88, 97
bowel habit, 12, 107
brain, 17, 19, 22, 109
brainwaves pattern, 161, 165
breast cancer, 102
breast tenderness, 112
breathing, 28, 93, 163
– chest, 22
– controlled, 23
– deep, 22, 23, 24, 27, 35
– diaphragm, 22
– exercises, 24, 167
– overbreathing, 22, 23, 118
– patterns, 23
– rapid, 22, 23
– rate, 161
– relaxed, 22, 23, 27
– rhythmical, 24
– shallow, 22, 23
– slow, 80
breathlessness, 17, 22, 101
British Association for Counselling, 137 *et seq.*
British Diabetic Association, 103

British Holistic Medical Association, 23, 132
British Medical Acupuncture Society, 132
British Medical Association, 40
British Migraine Association, 110
British Tinnitus Association, 115
British Wheel of Yoga, 168
bronchi, 13, 34, 101
Buddhism, 158, 159
bullying at school, 58
burglary, 83
burn-out, 87, 93
bus conductors, 89

calcium blocker, 100
callisthenics, 169
calmness, 23, 24, 158, 162
cancer, 33, 34, 90, 102, 103, 121, 127
career, 48, 50, 51, 63, 87, 89, 90, 151
Careline, 61
Catholic Marriage Advisory Council, 54
Centre for autogenic training, 161
chain smoking, 35
changes, 40, 41, 47, 86, 96
– physiological, 14, 33, 167
– psychological, 9, 10, 53, 95
chest discomfort, 15, 16, 17
child, death of, 9
child guidance, 58
childbearing, 51
childhood, 57–62
ChildLine, 62
children, 47, 50, 55, 57, 63, 65, 66, 67, 70, 73, 74, 78, 80, 98, 104, 147
choking, 18, 22
Christmas, 41
chronic illness, 42, 103
chronic pain, 15
church activities, 40, 56, 60, 170
cigarettes, 33, 34, 35, 104, 106, *see also* smoking
cities, 76, 78
citizens advice bureaux, 46, 70, 83, 96, 135, 139
City of London Migraine Clinic, 110
claustrophobia, 82
clinical psychologist, 127

clinics, 110, 124
– family planning, 49
– sex, 49
clumsiness, 112
coffee, 17, 22, 35, 82
colon, 108
communication, 55, 73, 86, 89, 94, 132, 137
commuters, 77, 78, 89
Compassionate Friends, 45
complementary medicine, 131 et seq.
compulsive fasting, 32
concentration, 34, 36, 68, 80, 86, 118, 160
conciliation, 67, 70
confidant, 43, 134, 136, 142
conflict, 36, 47, 50, 51, 52, 53, 63, 64, 67, 68, 89, 90, 152, 153, 164
Conquering Your Agoraphobia, 119
constipation, 18, 107, 121
Conversation by correspondence through friends by post, 72
coping, 10, 43, 57, 60, 73, 86, 93, 125, 127, 132, 142, 145–152, 155, 164
Coronary Prevention Group, 105
cortisol, 13, 88
cough and smoking, 34
Council for Acupuncture, 132
Council for voluntary service, 98, 139
counselling, 46, 49, 53, 54, 61, 62, 66, 71, 77, 92, 96, 101, 112, 129, 134, 135–141
courses, 94
– assertion, 73
– smoking cessation, 36
courts of law, 70, 77, 84, 89, 96
crime, 83–85, 95
Crohn's disease, 108
Cruse Bereavement Care, 45
crying, 112

deafness, 42
death, 40, 41, 43, 44, 66, 86, 95, 127
– of spouse, 9, 40, 63
debt-counselling, 96
defence mechanism, 146
delusions, 149
denying, 146, 147

dependence, 33, 123, 147
– alcohol, 37, 38, 171
– physical, 37
– psychological, 37
dependents, 73
depression, 16, 20, 32, 37, 44, 51, 65, 72, 96, 112, 116–128
Depressives Associated, 126
detachment, 144, 150
detoxification unit, 124
diabetes mellitus, 103, 104, 161
diarrhoea, 15, 18, 108, 118
diet, 105, 108, 112, 131, 170
disability, 16
– physical, 42
– psychological, 42
disablement, 42
discipline and children, 58, 59
disorientation, 65
displacement in divorce, 147
district nurse, 129
divorce, 9, 40, 54, 63, 64–70, 71, 86, 119, 145
dizziness, 107, 116
doctor, 18, 19, 20, 21, 22, 23, 36, 42, 44, 45, 46, 89, 104, 129–133, 136, 139, 161, 162, see also general practitioner
domestic chores, 50, 63, 90
domestic framework, 47
domestic friction, 146
dreamlike behaviour, 44, 142, 147
dreams, 29, 36
drinking, 31, 37, 63, 93, see also alcohol
Drinkwatchers handbook, 39
driving, 77, 78, 79, 80, 89
drop-in-centres, 56, 154
drowsiness, 20, 34
Drug and Therapeutics Bulletin, 107, 123, 189
drug dependence clinic, 124
drugs, 21, 43, 60, 92, 107, 108, 111, 122, 124, 132
– pain-killing, 43
duodenal ulcer (see ulcer)

earplugs, 21
eating pattern, 32, 33, 35, 41, 63, 80, 92, 97, 100, 110, 112, 132

eczema, 114
education, 23, 39, 132, 137
elderly *see* older people
emotions/emotional reactions, 10, 12, 19, 21, 33, 43, 47, 51, 53, 60, 66, 90, 102
employees, 89, 91
employer, 89, 91, 92
endoscopy, 111
environment, 131, 132, 151, 153, 159, 163
envy, 48
epilepsy, 181
exams, 24, 59, 158
executives, 88, 90, 93, 146
exercise, 16, 17, 22, 34, 43, 97, 100, 105, 106, 131, 162–167
exhaustion, 25, 96
expectations, 47, 54, 63, 170
Exploring Parenthood, 51
extramarital relationships, 49
extrovert, 32, 37
eyes, 13, 87

factory workers, 87
failure, 54, 64, 71, 149, 150
fainting, 17
Families Anonymous, 125
Families under stress, 56
family, 11, 34, 37, 38, 40, 43, 47, 51, 52, 53, 54, 55, 57, 63, 70, 74, 85, 89, 91, 92, 101, 103, 120, 133, 150, 151, 152, 170
family planning clinics, 49
family practitioner committee, 130
fatigue, 19, 25, 34, 36, 78, 106, 112
fear, 43, 60, 69, 88, 100, 118
Fellowship of Depressives Anonymous, 126
fibrositis, 25
financial state, 16, 40, 42, 48, 50, 51, 52, 54, 63, 66, 74, 80, 83, 90, 95, 96, 97, 139
flying, 15, 82, 158
fostering, 51
Freephone Drug Problems, 124
Friedman and Rosenman, 105
friends, 38, 40, 43, 45, 55, 69, 120, 127, 133, 170

frigidity, 49
frustration, 51, 92

gardening, 171
gastric acid, 14
gastric ulcer (*see* ulcer)
gastro-intestinal tract, 12, 18
genetic factors, 101, 105, 106, 114
gifted child, 59
Gingerbread, 70
glyceryl trinitrate, 100
God, 44, 153
GP, 21, 36, 49, 119, 122, 127, 129–133, 134, 139, *see also* doctor
grief, 44–46, 67, 69, 139
guilt, 43, 65, 69

habit, 23, 33, 39, 41, 63
handicap, 42, 51, 63
hay fever, 99, 114
head, 27, 28, 29, 30
headache, 15, 25, 34, 106, 109, 110, 112, 118, 120, 158
health, 34, 40, 42, 43, 86
– visitor, 46, 129
Healthcall, 130
Healthline, 130
heart attack, 17, 33, 34, 42, 88, 90, 92, 95, 103, 104, 106, 161
heart rate, 12, 14, 16, 17, 77, 131, 159, 161, 165
help, 53, 69, 73, 127, 134–141, 153
help from others, 127, 134–141
helping oneself, 69, 142–154
helping others, 151, 152
histamine, 99
HMSO, 84, 92
hobbies, 120, 147, 171, 172, *see also* pastimes.
holiday, 9, 35, 41, 42, 63, 71, 80–83, 92, 95
holistic medicine, 132 *et seq.*
Holmes and Rahe, 40
hormones, 13, 14, 15, 88, 100, 102, 104
hospital, 23, 49, 98, 108, 124, 128, 141, 147, 166
hostility, 53, 54, 79, 86, 105, 144
Housing Debtline, 96
hydrocortisone, 13, 88

hypertension, 105, 106, 107, 156, *see also* blood pressure
hyperventilation, 22
hypnotherapy, 162, 163
hypochondria, 16, 120

illness, 9, 10, 11, 16, 18, 21, 32, 35, 40, 41, 42, 43, 44, 59, 63, 74, 89, 99, 103, 118, 125, 148
– chronic, 42, 103
immune system, 99, 102, 113
imprisonment, 9 (*see also* jail term)
impulsiveness, 86
in-laws, 40
incontinence, 18
indigestion, 18, 111
infidelity, marital, 49
injury, 41, 88
insomnia, 20, 21, 34, 36, 121
Institute for the Study of Drug Dependence, 125
Institute of marital studies, 54
interests, 20, 63, 72, 74, 151
interview, 24, 53, 54
introvert, 32, 37
involuntary nervous system, 160
irritability, 32, 33, 34, 37, 54, 55, 75, 78, 86, 87, 112, 120, 146
irritable bowel syndrome, 107, 108
itching, 99

jail term, 9, 40, 41, 84 *et seq.*
jaw, 79, 100
jealousy, sibling, 57, 63
jet lag, 82, 88
Jewish Marriage Council, 53
job
– change of, 9, 10, 145
– ill-paid, 83
– loss, 40, 41, 50, *see also* unemployment
joints, 99, 112, 113

keep fit, 35, 167

laughter, 171
law, 41, 60, 63, 66, 71, 83
leisure, 11, 95, 167, 168, 171, 172
lethargy, 20
life events, 9, 40, 82, 119, 126

Lifeskills, 158
listening, 137, 143, *see also* counselling
loneliness, 71, 72
loss, 44, 65, 66, 69, 116, 119, 153
love, 68, 158
lugubriousness, 32
lumbago, 25
lungs, 100

marital infidelity, 49, 63
marital problems, 53, 95, 134, 146, 147
marital separation, 40, 41
– reconciliation, 40
marriage, 9, 10, 11, 40, 41, 42, 47–54, 63, 64, 66, 67, 69
marriage guidance, 49, 53, 69, 134, 139
massage, 25, 26–31, 93, 131
maturity, 48, 60, 67
mediation, 77
meditation, 132, 155, 158–160
menopause, 73
menstruation, 112
Mental Health Foundation, 62, 92, 136
mental illness, 125, 129
Message Home, 62
metabolic balance, 13, 23
metabolic rate, 161
mid-life crisis, 74
middle-age, 20, 73, 74, *see also* older people
migraine, 93, 109, 110
Migraine Trust, 109, 110
MIND, 73, 121
mortgage, 10, 40
mother and toddler groups, 56
motivation, 87, 95, 162
motorists (*see* driving)
mourning, 45, 65, 69
muscles, 12, 13, 15, 18, 19, 24, 25, 78, 79, 80, 88, 100, 104, 155, 157, 158, 165, 172
– tension, 12, 14, 22, 25, 26, 166
music, 63, 76, 77, 131, 172

Narcotics Anonymous, 125

Nat. Association for Premenstrual Syndrome, 113
Nat. Association of Victims Support Schemes, 83
Nat. Association of Widows, 45, 46
Nat. Association of Young People's Counselling & Advisory Services, 61, 62
Nat. Children's Home, 61
Nat. Council for Carers and their Elderly Dependents, 73
Nat. Council for One Parent Families, 70
Nat. Council for the Divorced and Separated, 70
Nat. Council for Voluntary Organisations, 98
Nat. Diabetes Foundation, 104
Nat. Drinkwatchers Network, 39
Nat. Eczema Society, 114
Nat. Family Conciliation Council, 70
Nat. Federation of Solo Clubs, 71
Nat. Institute of Medical Herbalists, 132
Nat. Retreat Centre, 154
Nat. Society of Non-smokers, 36
nausea, 18
NCH Careline, 61
neck, 27, 28, 29, 31, 79, 100
– ache, 158
neighbours, 45, 63, 77
nervous system, 14, 23
nicotine, 33, see also smoking
noise, 15, 21, 76, 77, 82, 86, 116
noradrenaline, 13, 14, 33, 100, 102, 104
Northern Ireland Regional Unit, 124
Northern Ireland Women's Aid, 56
nurses, 44, 129
nutrition, 11, 113, 158, 170

obsession, 142, 143
occupational therapist, 27
oesophageal ulcer (see ulcer)
older people, 20, 32, 63, 73–75, 82, 83, 98, 126, 128, 147, 148
Open Door Association, 119
Organisation for Parents under Stress, OPUS, 56
Outsiders Club, 72

overbreathing, 22, 23
overcrowding, 63, 75, 84
overwork, 87, 92, 93

pain, 15, 16, 17, 21, 25, 26, 28, 29, 31, 43, 64, 99, 100, 127, 170
– abdominal, 18
– ulcer, 18, 112
painkillers, 25
palpitations, 15, 16, 17, 34, 107, 118
panic, 23, 32, 112, 118, 126
paranoia, 144, 147
Parent Lifeline, 56
parents, 45, 48, 51, 52, 55, 56, 57, 58, 59, 60, 61, 63, 67, 68, 69, 71, 73
Parents Anonymous (London), 56
part-time work, 97
partner, 47, 49, 50, 51, 53, 54, 65, 66
pastimes, 92, see also hobbies, 92
peptic ulcer (see ulcer)
personal injury, 40
personality traits, 32, 75, 79, 87, 105, 119, 132, 142, 143
personnel officer, 92
pessimism, 32, 116
pets, 152
phobia, 118 et seq.
Phobics Society, 119
phone (see telephone)
phone-in, 70, 130, 136
physiotherapist, 23, 27, 129
placebo, 132
police, 83, 89
positive feelings, 34, 48, 163
positive stress, 11, 60
post-natal depression, 120
pre-menstrual syndrome, 112
– tension, 112
Pre-Menstrual Tension Advisory Service, 113
Pre-Retirement Association of Great Britain & Northern Ireland, 97
pregnancy, 40, 57, 63, 104
premature ejaculation, 49
progressive relaxation, 155 et seq.
Princess Margaret Migraine Clinic, 109
prison, 9, 40, 41, 84, 95
problem drinker, 37, 38, 39
professional advice, 58, 59, 69

projection, 146
protective mechanisms, 118
psoriasis, 115
Psoriasis Association, 115
psychiatrist, 127
psychoanalysis, 141
psychotherapy, 69, 140, 141, 161
pulse rate (*see* heart rate)

quarrelling, 24, 51
querulousness, 15

rash, 99
reconciliation, 65, 66
recreation, 41, 167–172
redundancy, 86, 89, 148
refuge, women's, 55
regression, 147
regret, 43, 64
RELATE Nat. Marriage Guidance
    Council, 53, 96
relationships, 11, 16, 32, 37, 38, 44,
    45, 47, 48, 49, 51, 58, 67, 68, 72,
    87, 90, 91, 92, 103, 126, 134, 139,
    140, 141, 142, 147, 151, 152, 153
relatives, 23, 45, 69, 73, 126, 127
relaxation, 20, 22, 23, 25, 26, 27, 28,
    33, 35, 36, 80, 82, 105, 107, 109,
    112, 123, 129, 132, 152, 154,
    155–156, 167, 170, 172
Relaxation for living, 158
Release, 125
religion, 136, 153, 154, 170
resentment, 44, 50, 54
resourcefulness, 75
rest, 20
restlessness, 34
retreats, 153
rheumatoid arthritis, 113, 114, 131
role-playing, 164
roles, 47, 50, 52, 87, 89
ROSPA, 89
row, 24
runaway children, 62

sadness, 43, 44, 64, 120
saliva, 12, 18
Samaritans, 127, 128, 136
school, 41, 50, 58, 59, 63, 68
– phobia, 59
Scottish Drugs Forum, 124

Scottish Marriage Guidance
    Council, 54
Scottish Women's Aid, 55
security, 57, 68, 71, 143, 147, 148
sedatives, 122
Self Health, 20, 109, 167, 189
self
– assurance, 37
– confidence, 72, 94
– control, 169
– deception, 146
– demanding, 105
– doubt, 90
– expression, 172
– esteem, 73, 95, 147, 148
– harm, 127, 128
– help, 132
– hypnosis, 155, 162, 163
– image, 145
– perception, 148
– referral, 124
self-help groups, 11
separation, 40, 41, 50, 53, 64, 65, 67,
    68, 70, 72
– anxiety in, 58, 59, 67
Serving the second sentence, 85
sex, 22, 33, 36, 49, 55, 60, 86, 116,
    121, 134, 137, 139
– difficulties, 9, 40, 42, 49, 63, 65
shift-work, 21, 87, 88
shock, 24, 60, 61
shoulders, 27, 28, 29, 31, 79
shyness, 71, 72
side effects, 122
sighing, 22
singing, 171, 172
single parenthood, 51, 69, 70
skin disease, 114
sleep, 20, 21, 22, 25, 31, 36, 80, 121,
    159, 167, 170
– disturbed, 20, 92
– inadequate, 20, 55
– pattern, 36, 41, 63, 82
sleeping pills, 21, 36, 45, 122
smoking, 31, 33, 34, 36, 63, 104, 106,
    107, 111, 170
social
– activities, 41, 42
– climate, 47
– contacts, 45, 151
– drinkers, 37

– isolation, 97, 126
– pressures, 16
– problems, 63
– services, 51
– skills therapy, 71
social worker, 46, 69, 89, 136
Society of Teachers of the Alexander
   Technique, 26
Someone to talk to at work, 92
Someone to Talk to Directory, 62, 136
South Wales Association for the
   Prevention of Addiction, 125
spasm, muscle, 100, 107, 108, 109
spine, 28, 29
spouse, 34, 40, 41, 68, 75, 125, 127,
   134, 146, 170
stammering, 19
Standing Conference on Drug
   Abuse (SCODA), 124
step-parenting, 51
steroids, 108
stimulation, 15, 22, 33, 34, 35, 36, 97
stomach, 12
stress chart, 40, 64
– ratings, 40, 83
Stress Foundation, 94, 172
stress related disorders, 161, 165
stroke, 42, 105, 161
Student's Nightline, 62
submissive behaviour, 48, 72, 73, 96
suffocation, 22
suicide, 75, 95, 121, 126–128
surgery, 119, 131, 132
suspiciousness, 32, 75
sweating, 12, 14, 17, 20, 37, 116,
   118, 165, 166
sympathetic nervous system, 14

T'ai-Chi-Chuan, 169
tea, 17, 22, 35
teachers, 26, 58, 59, 88
technology, 86, 87, 93
teenagers, 32, 60, 63, *see also*
   adolescents
telephone, 80, 86, 128
tension, 12, 14, 19, 22, 23, 25, 26, 27,
   29, 30, 33, 35, 36, 49, 51, 64, 79,
   80, 96, 112, 117, 155, 157, 158, 169
The Vision, 154
tingling, 23
tinnitus, 115

tiredness, 17, 19, 20, 36, 51, 55, 80
tobacco, 34, 35, *see also* smoking
tooth-clenching, 25, 79
traffic, 21, 76, 77, 78, 80, 89
traffic wardens, 89
tranquillisers, 45, 112, 122–126, 129,
   136
TRANX (UK) Ltd (National
   Tranquilliser Advice Centre), 123
travel, 21, 80–83
trembling, 17, 19, 34
trinitrin, 100
truancy, 59, 60, 63
twitching, 19, 93
type A type B, 105

ulcer, 18, 90, 108, 110, 111
ulcerative colitis, 108
unconsciousness, 17
Understanding Cancer, 102, 185
Understanding Stress (HMSO), 92
unemployment, 11, 51, 55, 91, 95,
   96, 97, 119
urination, 18
urticaria, 114

values, 52, 60
vandalism, 60, 83
violence, 55, 63, 89
voluntary aftercare, 85
voluntary work, 46, 70, 89, 98, 128,
   129, 139, 151
Volunteer Centre, 98

walking, 21, 34, 36, 152
warning signs, 32 *et seq.*, 58, 59
weight gain, 32, 63
weight loss, 32, 107, 121
Welsh Women's Aid, 56
Westminster Pastoral Foundation,
   136
wheezing, 99, 101
Which?, 130, 133
widowed, 45, 46, 64, 71
widows advisory centres, 46
wife-battering, 55
withdrawal symptoms, 34, 37, 122,
   124
– clinics, 36
withdrawn, 143, 144, 147

Women's Aid Federation (England) Ltd, 55
work, 11, 36, 37, 40, 41, 42, 47, 48, 51, 53, 74, 80, 86–95, 118, 134, 146, 150, 151, 152
– ethic, 94
workaholic, 92, 93
workshops, 39, 46, 51, 94, 132, 154

worry, 15, 16, 67, 71

yoga, 35, 154, 167, 168
Yoga for Health Foundation, 168
young people, 38, 59, 61, 63, 72, 96,
   see also adolescents
Young Runaway's Project, 61
young wives' groups, 56

some other Consumer Publications

Renting and letting   £5.95

is a book which helps to clarify the legal position of all who pay
rent to occupy their home, and anyone who wants to let
property. The law of landlord and tenant is complex and
confers rights as well as responsibilities on both sides. The
book explains when a landlord cannot get vacant possession
from a tenant, and in what circumstances he can. It includes
sections on rent control and getting a fair rent registered,
explains the meaning of protected and statutory tenancy and
what happens on the death of the original tenant. It deals with
the repair obligation of landlords and the various protections a
tenant has, including protection from harassment and eviction
and explains the council tenant's rights, including the right to
buy the rented property. (England and Wales, not Scotland.)

Which? way to buy, sell and move house   £9.95

takes you through all the stages of moving to another home –
considering the pros and cons of different places, house hunt-
ing, viewing, having a survey, making an offer, getting a
mortgage, completing the purchase, selling the present home.
It explains the legal procedures and the likely costs. Buying
and selling at auction and in Scotland are specifically dealt
with. The practical arrangements for the move and for any
repairs or improvements to the new house are described.
Advice is given for easing the tasks of sorting, packing and
moving possessions, people and pets, with a removal firm or
by doing it yourself, and for making the day of the move go
smoothly.

What to do after an accident   £5.95

explains your legal rights when another person's negligence
has caused you harm and how to set about claiming compensa-

tion. It deals with accidents on the road (as driver, passenger, pedestrian, cyclist), at home (your own or someone else's), at work, when out and about. The book provides guidance on court proceedings, negotiating through lawyers, assessing damages, making insurance claims, applying for statutory payments. There is also advice on medical treatment and coping with disability and getting back to work, with the names of organisations providing help and support.

Approaching retirement   £6.95

will help you prepare for a happy and rewarding retirement. It tells you when to start planning for it (probably earlier than you think), how to adapt to having more free time, what benefits and concessions you will get, and how to cope financially. There is information about pensions, from the state or an employer, and tax, about how to find work in retirement, about organising your finances to provide an income and minimise your tax bill. The book also advises on the decision whether to move or stay put, on keeping well, and on adjusting to a different daily routine.

Making the most of higher education   £6.95

is a practical guide for both the 18+ student and the mature student, giving advice about choosing subjects and courses (with an eye to career prospects), getting a place at a university, polytechnic or other college, applications and interviews. It also advises on ways of studying effectively towards a degree, making ends meet on a grant, planning for a career, and many other student problems.

Earning money at home   £6.95

explains how to brush up a skill or hobby into a money-making venture. It gives advice on organising your family and domestic life, on advertising your activities, costing and selling your work, dealing with customers. There is information on statutory and financial requirements for insurance, tax, accounts, VAT, employing others. The book suggests ways in which your experience from a previous job could be utilised, or a skill or hobby developed to a professional standard, or how unexploited energy and ability can be used profitably. Suggestions are made for improving your skills to a higher standard, and the names and addresses are given of organisations that might be helpful.

Starting your own business £6.95

for people who have the courage, imagination and stamina to try a new venture on their own, this is a competent guide to help them through the essential steps. It advises on defining precisely what product or skill you have to offer, how to raise the necessary capital and cope with legal requirements. It deals with all the financial aspects: pricing the product, calculating overheads and cash flow, keeping accounts and other records, dealing with taxes including VAT, marketing and selling, premises and insurance. Throughout, sources of advice and information are given to help the small businessman make a success of going it alone.

Understanding cancer £5.95

explains the nature and causes of the disease most people find more frightening than any other. It tells you how to recognise some of the symptoms and avoid some of the risks, and explains how cancer is diagnosed. It goes into the details of various forms of treatment: surgery, radiotherapy, chemotherapy, including their possible side effects, and takes an objective look at the role of alternative/complementary therapies. It describes some of the advances in cancer research but does not pretend that these will soon provide the long awaited cure. The book deals with advanced cancer and terminal care but stresses that cancer must not be regarded as inevitably fatal.

Children, parents and the law £5.95

describes the legal responsibilities and rights of a parent, and
of a child towards parents, so far as they exist. It deals with
illegitimacy, when things go wrong in the family, with education, if a child comes up against the law, when a child has to go
into the care of the local authority, and explains what is
involved in custodianship, guardianship, adoption, fostering.
It sets out at what ages a child can carry out specific activities –
from buying a pet to getting married. There is a section
explaining the effects of a child being injured and of the death
of one or both parents.

Wills and probate £6.95

is a layman's guide on how to make your will without employing a solicitor and how to administer the estate of someone
who has died. For making a will, it tells you how to assess your
likely estate, what to consider when appointing executors and
a guardian for children. It shows you how to ensure that your
will is free from ambiguity: what to say and how to say it, so
that your wishes can be carried out without complication, how
a will should be signed and witnessed and what to do when
you wish to alter your will. It explains the implications of
inheritance tax and capital gains tax and points out where and
how tax can be saved.

  For someone called upon to act as an executor, the probate
section of the book is a step-by-step guide through the procedure, including sections on calculating the assets, how to get
and fill in the probate forms, carrying out valuations, dealing
with the bank and what to do while the accounts of the
deceased are frozen, paying inheritance tax and dealing with
income tax and capital gains tax, and all the other tasks that
need to be performed in order to get a grant of probate. After
probate has been granted, the executor has to deal with
transferring property, selling or transferring shares, encashing
national savings, gathering in the assets and distributing the
legacies and bequests to beneficiaries.

The book also explains what happens, and what has to be done, if there is no will and the next of kin have to cope with the administration.

What to do when someone dies £6.95

is a companion volume to *Wills and probate*. It aims to help those who have never had to deal with the arrangements that must be made after a death – getting a doctor's certificate and registering the death, deciding whether to bury or cremate, choosing an undertaker and a coffin, putting notices in the papers, selecting the form of service, claiming national insurance benefits. It explains the function of people with whom they will come in contact, often for the first time. They will get help and guidance from the doctor, the registrar, the undertaker, the clergyman, the cemetery or crematorium officials, the Department of Health and Social Security and, in some circumstances, the police and the coroner. However, it is the executor or nearest relative who has to make the decisions, often at a time of personal distress. The book describes what needs to be done, when, and how to set about it.

No attempt is made to deal with the personal or social aspects of death, such as the psychology of grief and shock, the rituals and conventions of mourning, or attitudes to death.

Taking your own case to court or tribunal £3.95

is for people who do not have a solicitor to represent them in a county court or magistrates' court or before a tribunal. This book tells you the procedures to follow in preparing and presenting your case, what happens at the hearing, what steps can be taken to enforce a judgment, how to appeal if the judgment goes against you. It explains in layman's terms how to conduct proceedings yourself in the county court (arbitration for 'small claims' and open court hearings), in the High Court (rarely appropriate for a litigant-in-person), in a magistrates' court (for both civil and criminal matters), at a social security appeal tribunal (challenging a DHSS benefits decision) and before an industrial tribunal (dismissal cases).

Divorce – legal procedures and financial facts £6.95

explains the special procedure for an undefended divorce and deals with the financial facts to be faced when a marriage ends in divorce. Aspects covered include getting legal advice, conciliation, legal aid and its drawbacks, the various financial and property orders the court can make, what can happen to the matrimonial home, the children, how to calculate needs and resources, the effect of tax, coping with shortage of money after divorce.

Each couple faces different problems: the book illustrates the effects of alternative financial solutions to various personal situations on divorce.

Consumer Publications are available from Consumers' Association, Castlemead, Gascoyne Way, Hertford SG14 1LH, and from booksellers.

OTHER CA PUBLICATIONS INCLUDE:

The Drug and Therapeutic Bulletin £23 p.a.

is a fortnightly broadsheet published by the Consumers'
Association mainly for the medical profession and pharma-
cists. In it, named drugs are assessed and the latest research on
effects, side effects and therapeutic use are concisely sum-
marised. The *Drug and Therapeutics Bulletin* helps prescribers
keep up-to-date with developments in drug therapy. It can be
read in minutes. Like all CA's publications, the *Drug and
Therapeutics Bulletin* is independent of manufacturers and carries no advertisements.

Self Health £12 p.a.

is a quarterly health and food magazine; based on the same
principles as *Which?* It is independent, unbiased and accepts
no advertising. Free from commercial pressures, it can give
honest and unbiased information. The magazine is produced
by the College of Health and written by independent jour-
nalists, doctors, surgeons, academics, and health and nutrition
experts who will give you the straight facts without bias and
without confusing you with medical or technical jargon.

Following in the tradition of *Which?*, *Self Health* frequently
takes a close look behind the health scene, exposing bad
practice and harmful products in order to prevent the consumer, from being deceived.